THE SCHOOL MATHEMATICS PROJECT

BOOK B

CAMBRIDGE UNIVERSITY PRESS

Cambridge
London   New York   New Rochelle
Melbourne   Sydney

THE SCHOOL MATHEMATICS PROJECT

When the SMP was founded in 1961, its main objective was to devise radically new secondary school mathematics courses to reflect, more adequately than did the traditional syllabuses, the up-to-date nature and usages of mathematics. The first texts produced embodied new courses for O-level (*SMP Books 1–5*) and A-level (*SMP Advanced Mathematics Books 1–4*). *Books 3, 4* and *5* have now been revised to become *SMP New Book 3, Parts 1* and *2, New Book 4, Parts 1* and *2*, and *New Book 5*, while *Revised Advanced Mathematics Books 1, 2* and *3* cover the syllabus for the A-level examination in SMP Mathematics. Five shorter texts cover the material of the various sections of the A-level examination SMP Further Mathematics. There are two books for SMP Additional Mathematics at O-level. All the SMP GCE examinations are available to schools through any of the GCE examining boards.

Books A–H cover broadly the same development of mathematics as the first few books of the O-level series. Most CSE boards offer appropriate examinations. In practice this series is being used very widely across all streams of comprehensive schools and its first seven books, together with *Books X, Y* and *Z*, provide a course leading to the SMP O-level examination. *SMP Cards I* and *II* provide an alternative treatment in card form of the mathematics in *Books A–D*. The six Units of *SMP 7–13*, designed for children in that age-range, provide a course for middle schools which is also widely used in primary schools and the first two years of secondary schools. Teacher's Guides accompany all these series.

The SMP has produced many other texts and teachers are encouraged to obtain each year from Cambridge University Press, The Edinburgh Building, Shaftesbury Road, Cambridge CB2 2RU, the full list of SMP publications currently available. In the same way, help and advice may always be sought by teachers from the Executive Director at the SMP Office, Westfield College, Kidderpore Avenue, London NW3 7ST.

The annual Reports, details of forthcoming in-service training courses, SMP syllabuses and other information may be obtained from the same address.

The SMP is continually evaluating old work and preparing for new. The effectiveness of the SMP's work depends, as it has always done, on the comments and reactions received from a wide variety of teachers – and also from pupils – using SMP materials. Readers of the texts can, therefore, send their comments to the SMP in the knowledge that they will be valued and carefully studied.

Preface

This is the second of eight books designed to cover a course suitable for those who wish to take a CSE Examination on one of the reformed mathematics syllabuses.

The material is based upon the first four books of the O-level series, SMP Books 1–4. The connection is maintained to the extent that it will be possible to change from one series to the other at the end of the first year or even at a later stage. For example, having started with Books A and B, a pupil will be able to move to Book 2. Within each year's work, the material has been entirely broken down and rewritten.

The differences between this Main School series and the O-level series have been explained at length in the Preface to Book A as have the differences between the content of these two SMP courses and that of the more traditional text.

In this book, Book B, and in the remainder of the series, metric units are used. Money is in pounds and new pence; length in metres and also centimetres and kilometres; weight is in grammes and kilogrammes. Measures of time and angle remain unchanged.

The Prelude introduces work that is preliminary to the tessellation and area chapters. It is concerned with patterns that fill the plane. The chapter on tessellation then concentrates upon the properties of angle and side necessary in polygons that tessellate while the area chapter concentrates upon measurement by comparison with any unit area.

There are two other geometry chapters. One concerns the application of the idea of angle to bearing and direction. The other introduces the study of transformations. In later books we shall meet transformations which preserve distance and shape, as we did in a preliminary way in the symmetry chapter of Book A. We shall also meet transformations such as enlargement and shearing, but in this book we consider a transformation that preserves neither shape nor size, but only properties of containment, order and incidence.

The decimals chapter is really about measurement, the difficulty of obtaining and expressing accurate measurements and of stating the degree of accuracy. It relies heavily upon the experience of place value developed in the number base chapter of Book A. The number base chapter of this book concentrates less upon place value than upon the applications of binary arithmetic.

The fractions chapter continues the efforts started in Book A, to make fractions more completely understood without stressing manipulation. A chapter on directed numbers introduces the signs $(^+)$ and $(^-)$ as generalizations

Preface

of 'above, below', 'before, after', etc. Directed numbers as shifts will be discussed in Book C.

There are two algebra chapters: one on the meaning of letters in a mathematical context; (equations are not discussed; the emphasis is upon the meaning of a symbol 'for all x in the set S...' and the formation of simple formulae); the other on relations, mappings and ordered pairs.

Answers to exercises are not printed at the end of this book but are contained in the companion Teacher's Guide which gives a detailed commentary on the pupil's text. In this series, the answers and commentary are interleaved with the pupil's text.

ACKNOWLEDGEMENTS

The principal authors, on whose contributions the S.M.P. texts are largely based, are named in the annual Reports. Many other authors have also provided original material, and still more have been directly involved in the revision of draft versions of chapters and books. The Project gratefully acknowledges the contributions which they and their schools have made.

This book—*Book B*—has been prepared by

J. K. Brunton   W. Mrozowski
Joyce Harris   Margaret Wilkinson
K. Lewis

and edited by P. G. Bowie assisted by Elizabeth Evans.

We would especially thank Dr J. V. Armitage for the advice he has given on the fundamental mathematics of the course.

Many other schoolteachers have been directly involved in the further development and revision of the material and the Project gratefully acknowledges the contribution which they and their schools have made.

The drawings at the chapter openings in this book are by Penny Wager

The Project is grateful to the Royal Mint for supplying the photographs of the coins which appear in Chapter 3.

We are much indebted to the Cambridge University Press for their cooperation and help at all times in the preparation of this book.

The Project owes a great deal to its Secretary. Miss A. J. Freeman; also to Mrs E. L. Humphreys and Mrs E. Muir for their assistance and for their typing in connection with this book.

Contents

Contents

Prelude

TILING PATTERNS

A kitchen or bathroom floor is sometimes covered with tiles all of the same shape and size. The tiles do not overlap and are fitted together without gaps where dirt could collect.

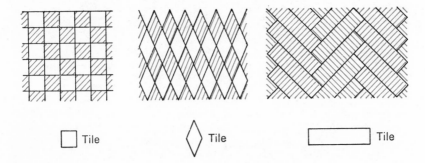

☐ Tile   ◇ Tile   ▭ Tile

Experiment 1

Equipment: tracing paper, thin card, scissors.
Trace this shape carefully. Use your tracing to help you to cut out triangles having the same shape and size. Try to get as many as possible from your card.
Make some interesting shapes with your triangles.
Can you use your triangles to make a tiling pattern?

Right-angled triangle

1

Experiment 2

Equipment: tracing paper, thin card, scissors.
Repeat Experiment 1 for each of the following shapes.

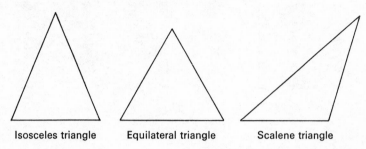

Isosceles triangle   Equilateral triangle   Scalene triangle

Draw a triangle of any shape you choose. Can you use it to make a tiling pattern? Do you think it is possible to form a tiling pattern from any triangle?

Experiment 3

Equipment: a nine-by-nine pinboard, spotty paper.

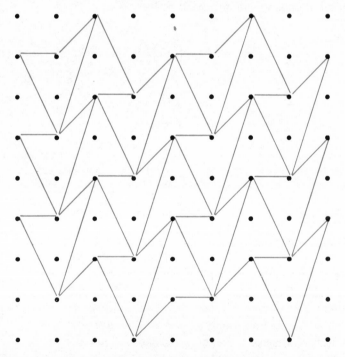

Pinboards can be used to make tiling patterns.

Form tiling patterns from each of the following quadrilaterals. (They are all quadrilaterals, but some of them have some regularity and these are given special names.) Record your results on spotty paper.

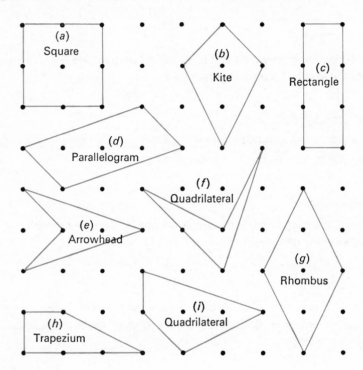

Experiment 4

Here is a tiling pattern formed from quadrilaterals.

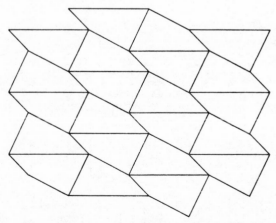

Trace it and colour all the tiles that are this way up.

Prelude

Do you think that any quadrilateral can be used to make a tiling pattern? Choose a difficult quadrilateral and find out whether a tiling pattern can be formed from it.

Experiment 5

Find a pentagon which will form a tiling pattern. Are there any pentagons which will not form tiling patterns?

Experiment 6

Find a hexagon which will form a tiling pattern. Are there any hexagons which cannot be used to make tiling patterns?

Experiment 7

There are many polygons which cannot be used to form a tiling pattern. How many can you find?

Class project

Look through newspapers and magazines to see how many actual tiling patterns you can find. Make a collection of them and display them in your classroom.

Experiment 8

Find out which of these shapes can be used to form tiling patterns.

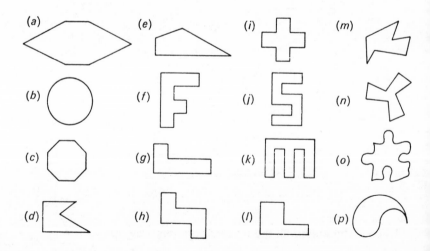

Experiment 9

It is possible to make a larger equilateral
triangle with four equilateral triangles of the
same size and shape.
Find other shapes which have this property.
Can you form tiling patterns from all of
these shapes?

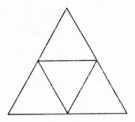

Experiment 10

Figures which have the same size and the same shape are called *congruent*
figures.
If you have a large supply of congruent equilateral triangles, you can
make a larger equilateral triangle from 4 triangles. Can you make a larger
equilateral triangle with any other number of triangles?
Experiment with other shapes.

Experiment 11

Tiles *A* and *B* together form a shape with rotational symmetry.
Find the centre of rotational symmetry.
How can tile *A* be moved about this centre so that it occupies the
position of tile *B*?
Can tile *A* be moved in this way so that it occupies the position of:
(i) tile *C*; (ii) tile *D*; (iii) tile *E*, (iv) tile *G*? Where are the centres of
symmetry?
How can: (i) tile *D*; (ii) tile *E* be moved so that it occupies the position
of tile *F*?
Have you found any other tiling patterns in which two tiles could be
moved to each other's position in this way?

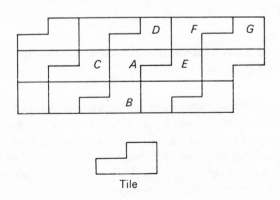

Tile

1. Letters for numbers

1. PATTERNS AMONG NUMBERS

(*a*)

These arrangements of dots both represent the rectangle number 8. They show that

$$4 \times 2 = 2 \times 4.$$

Are the following correct

(i) $9 \times 17 = 17 \times 9$;

(ii) $5 \times 8 = 8 \times 5$;

(iii) $3 \times 405 = 405 \times 3$?

Let *a* and *b* stand for any two members of the set of counting numbers. Is it always true that

$$a \times b = b \times a?$$

The use of letters helps us to say something about *all* the members of a set without listing every single one of them. In this case, they are 'substitutes' or 'stand ins' or 'understudies' for counting numbers. (Because of this, they can be joined with signs like '+' and '×' and '=' as though they really were numbers.) They stand for counting numbers until a particular counting number replaces them.

(*b*)

The dots show that
$$12 + 15 = 27.$$

From the arrangements of the dots,
$$(3 \times 4) + (3 \times 5) = (3 \times 9).$$

Noticing the red line
$$(3 \times 9) = 3 \times (4 + 5),$$

so
$$(3 \times 4) + (3 \times 5) = 3 \times (4 + 5).$$

Write down a similar expression for each of the following arrangements of dots:

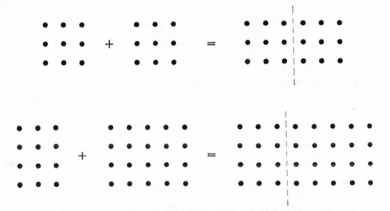

Set down an arrangement of dots for each of the following:
$$(2 \times 5) + (2 \times 7) = 2 \times (5 + 7);$$
$$(9 \times 1) + (9 \times 8) = 9 \times (1 + 8).$$

The arrangement of dots shows us one use of brackets. The numbers set out with the signs and brackets form a pattern. Is the pattern the same for all counting numbers? Can you use letters to show this pattern?

If *a*, *b* and *c* are members of the set of counting numbers, then this pattern is shown as
$$(a \times b) + (a \times c) = a \times (b + c).$$

7

Exercise A

In this exercise, the letters *a, b, c, d* stand for members of the set of counting numbers.

1 Use letters to show the following patterns:

(*a*) $6+12 = 12+6$
$1+3 = 3+1$
....

(*b*) $2 \times 3 = 3 \times 2$
$10 \times 9 = 9 \times 10$
....

(*c*) $(2+3)+4 = 2+3+4$
$(5+7)+8 = 5+7+8$
....

(*d*) $(5 \times 3) \times 6 = 5 \times (3 \times 6)$
$(6 \times 1) \times 2 = 6 \times (1 \times 2)$
....

(*e*) $(3+4) \times 2 = (3 \times 2)+(4 \times 2)$
$(7+2) \times 3 = (7 \times 3)+(2 \times 3)$
....

(*f*) $8+(6-2) = (8+6)-2$
$5+(4-3) = (5+4)-3$
....

2 Substitute numbers in each of the following. Work out each side of the equations you get and say which patterns are wrong for counting numbers.

(*a*) $a+b = b+a$;

(*b*) $a+b+b = b+a+b$;

(*c*) $a-b = b-a$;

(*d*) $a-b+b = b-b+a$;

(*e*) $a \times (b+c) = (b+c) \times a$;

(*f*) $a \times (b-c) = (b-c) \times a$;

(*g*) $(a-b)-c = a-(b-c)$;

(*h*) $a+b+c+d = d+c+b+a$.

3 Make up some letter patterns like those of Question 2. Write down five of them, of which three are correct for counting numbers and two are wrong.

2. SETS AND SUBSETS

2.1 Non-numerical sets

We have been talking about sets of numbers. The word 'set' can be used for collections of other things besides numbers. For example: the set of people who live in your house; the set of people who have sailed round the world alone; the set of chairs in your classroom; the set of points that make a certain line of symmetry; the set of objects in your pocket.

Exercise B

1 List the members of the following sets:

   (*a*) {the colours of a set of traffic lights};

   (*b*) {the subjects on your timetable};

   (*c*) {the days of the week};

   (*d*) {the letters of your surname};

   (*e*) {the five continents}.

2 Give a description which defines the following sets:

   (*a*) {£, p};

   (*b*) {hearts, clubs, diamonds, spades};

   (*c*) {a, e, i, o, u};

   (*d*) {sight, hearing, smell, touch, taste};

   (*e*) {September, April, June, November}.

3 Are the following statements true or false?

   (*a*) A square is a member of the set of polygons.

   (*b*) The Earth is a member of the set of planets.

   (*c*) An oak is a member of the set of flowers.

   (*d*) Tennis is a member of the set of sports.

   (*e*) Manchester is a member of the set of cities of England.

4 You are a member of your family, generation, school, the set of people who possess a pencil or pen. Name six other sets of which you are a member.

2.2 Subsets

When the members of one set *A* are all taken from another set *B*, then *A* is called a subset of *B*. Your family is a subset of the set of people who live in your road. The cars you have seen on the roads form a subset of all the cars in the world. Even numbers are a subset of the set of counting numbers. {2, 3, 5} is a subset of {1, 2, 3, 4, 5, 6}.

Exercise C

1 Make a list of all the subsets of {1, 2, 3, 4} which have three members.

2 Which of the following are true?

   (*a*) {odd numbers} is a subset of {counting numbers};

   (*b*) {square numbers} is a subset of {rectangle numbers};

   (*c*) {multiples of ten} is a subset of {rectangle numbers}.

3   Write down the set which is the intersection of the sets

$$A = \{2, 4, 6, 8, 10\} \quad \text{and} \quad B = \{2, 4, 8, 16, 32, 64\}.$$

Is A a subset of B? Is the intersection set a subset of (i) A, (ii) B?

4   There are many subsets within a family. For example {married women}, {uncles}, {people under the age of 11}. Write down five more subsets.

Some of the subsets may intersect. For example, the subset {people under the age of 11} might intersect with the subset {cousins}. Make a list of three pairs of subsets that could not possibly intersect.

Summary

The word 'set' can be used for a collection of any objects providing we can decide whether or not any particular object belongs to that collection. There must be a list of members or a clear description of the collection.

When members of one set, A, are all members of another set, B, then A is a subset of B.

3. FORMULAE

The patterns mentioned in Section 1 were very general. They applied to all counting numbers.

As you found in Book A, there are many patterns which apply only to subsets of the counting numbers.

The questions in Exercise D show you how to look for these patterns and how to describe them by means of a general expression or formula.

Exercise D

In each of the following questions, copy down the patterns replacing the question marks by the appropriate numbers or letters. n is any member of the set of counting numbers.

1   *Even numbers:*

the 1st even number is 2×1;

the 2nd even number is 2×2;

the 3rd even number is $? \times 3$;

the 4th even number is $? \times ?$;

....

the nth even number is $?$.

2 *Odd numbers:*

the 1st odd number is $2 \times 1 - 1$;
the 2nd odd number is $2 \times 2 - 1$;
the 3rd odd number is $? \times 3 - ?$;
....
the nth odd number is   ?.

3 *Triangle numbers.*

(i) The difference between the 2nd and 1st triangle numbers is 2;
The difference between the 3rd and 2nd triangle numbers is 3;
The difference between the 4th and 3rd triangle numbers is ?;
....
The difference between the nth and $(n-1)$th triangle numbers is ?.

(ii) By arranging triangle numbers in this manner,

we found that

the 1st triangle number is $\dfrac{1 \times 2}{2}$;

the 2nd triangle number is $\dfrac{2 \times 3}{2}$;

the 3rd triangle number is $\dfrac{3 \times ?}{?}$;

....
the nth triangle number is   ?.

4 *Polyhedra.* Sketch a tetrahedron, a square-based pyramid, a cube and an octahedron. If V stands for the number of vertices, F for the number of faces and E for the number of edges, complete the following table:

	V	F	E
Tetrahedron	4	4	6
Square-based pyramid	?	?	?
Cube	?	?	?
Octahedron	?	?	?

Letters for numbers

There is a connection between the numbers *V*, *F* and *E*. Write it down as an equation. *V*, *F* and *E* are members of what set of numbers? What is the least possible value that each can have?

5 *Angles*. (i) Two anticlockwise rotations follow each other and the result is a complete turn. If the first is *a* turns and the second is *b* turns, write down an expression for this result. Are *a* and *b* members of the set of counting numbers? What counting number is *b* less than?

   (ii) If the rotations are measured in degrees, what counting number is *b* less than?

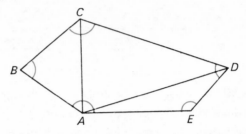

6 *Polygons*. (i) How many diagonals are there from any one vertex of

   (*a*) a 5-sided polygon;
   (*b*) a 6-sided polygon;
   (*c*) a 7-sided polygon;
   (*d*) an *n*-sided polygon?

   (ii) How many diagonals are there altogether in a 4-sided; 5-sided; 6-sided; 7-sided and 8-sided polygon?

   (iii)

   How many more diagonals has a 5-sided than a 4-sided polygon?
   How many more diagonals has a 6-sided than a 5-sided polygon?
   How many more diagonals has a 7-sided than a 6-sided polygon?
   How many more diagonals has an 8-sided than a 7-sided polygon?
   How many more diagonals has an *n*-sided than an (*n* − 1)-sided polygon?

2. Tessellations

1. PATTERN

On tracing paper, mark the vertices of the regular polygons shown in Figure 1. Prick through the tracing on to card. Join the vertices with straight lines and cut out the polygons. You can then draw round your polygons to produce as many as you need. Do not lose them; you will need them to help you to answer several questions in this chapter.

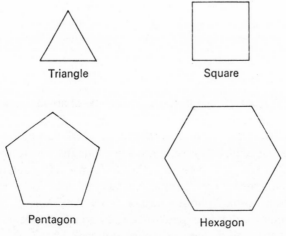

Triangle   Square

Pentagon   Hexagon

Fig. 1 (*a*)

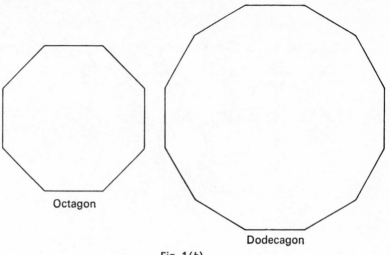

Octagon

Dodecagon

Fig. 1 (*b*)

(*a*) Take your equilateral triangles and fit them together to form the tiling pattern shown in Figure 2.

Imagine that you have an endless supply of triangles: could you continue the pattern to fill the whole plane?

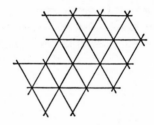

Fig. 2

(*b*) What size (in degrees) is each angle of an equilateral triangle?

(*c*) How many triangles fit round each vertex of the pattern?

(*d*) How many degrees are there in one whole turn?

(*e*) What is the connection between your answers to (*b*), (*c*) and (*d*)?

(*f*) Can you fit squares together to form a tiling pattern? How many degrees are there in each angle of a square? How many squares can you fit round a vertex without a gap or an overlap? Why?

Are you sure that your pattern can be continued indefinitely, supposing that you have an endless supply of squares?

Patterns which fill a plane are called *tessellations*. Figure 2 shows a tessellation of equilateral triangles.

(*g*) What size (in degrees) is each angle of a regular pentagon? Can you form a tessellation of regular pentagons? If you are not sure, try fitting your regular pentagons together.

(*h*) Can you form a tessellation of:

        (i)   regular hexagons;

        (ii) regular octagons;

        (iii) regular dodecagons?

Try to answer this question by thinking about the angles of these regular polygons. Check your decisions by fitting together your cut-out shapes.

(i) What is the smallest possible angle of a regular polygon?

List the set of factors of 360. How many factors are there? Compare your list with that of your neighbour. Which of your factors is the number of degrees in an angle of a regular polygon?

A tessellation of regular polygons, all of one kind and with their corners meeting at a point, is called a regular tessellation. How many regular tessellations do you think there are?

Exercise A

1 (*a*) Using squared paper to help you, copy and continue the patterns shown in Figure 3.

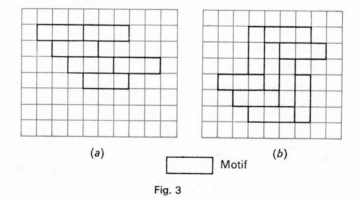

      (*a*)   (*b*)

☐ Motif

Fig. 3

(*b*) Draw a different tessellation of your own, using the same basic shape or motif.

(*c*) Where do you see tessellations of rectangles? Do the craftsmen who make them always use the same method? Look at the buildings which you pass on your way home.

15

2 (*a*) Copy and continue the patterns shown in Figure 4. Make sure that each pattern can be continued to fill the whole plane.

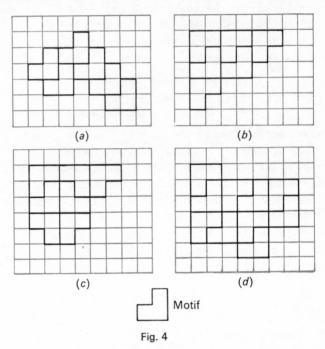

(*a*)　　　　(*b*)

(*c*)　　　　(*d*)

Motif

Fig. 4

(*b*) Colour your drawing of Figure 4 (*d*) so that shapes which are the same way up and the same way round are the same colour. How many colours do you need?

(*c*) Colour your drawing of Figure 4 (*c*) in the same way. How many colours do you need for this pattern?

3 (*a*) Using isometric graph paper to help you, copy and continue the patterns shown in Figure 5.

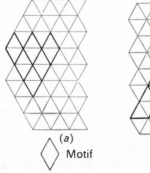

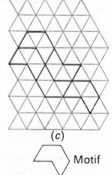

(*a*)
Motif

(*b*)
Motif

(*c*)
Motif

Fig. 5

(*b*) Draw at least two different tessellations for each of the three motifs.

4   The motif shown in Figure 6 is formed from a regular hexagon and an equilateral triangle. Use this motif to draw two different tessellations.

Fig. 6

5   Sketch a tessellation using the motif shown in Figure 7. Which two simple shapes are used to build this motif?

Fig. 7

6   (*a*) On a sheet of plain paper draw an accurate tessellation of regular hexagons. Use the method suggested by Figure 8.
     Are you satisfied with the appearance of your drawing? If not, do it again.

(*b*) Using as few colours as possible, colour your drawing so that no hexagon touches another hexagon of the same colour.

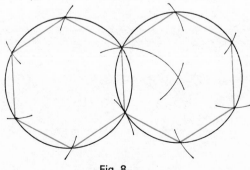

Fig. 8

17

7 Equipment: tracing paper, thin card, scissors.

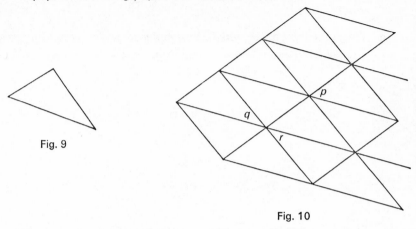

Fig. 9

Fig. 10

(*a*) Trace the triangle shown in Figure 9 on to card. Cut out triangles the same shape and the same size. Try to get as many as possible from your card. Paste about half your triangles into your exercise book to form the tessellation shown in Figure 10.

(*b*) Mark all the angles in your figure which are equal to the one marked with the letter *p*.

(*c*) What can you say about the angles marked with the letters *q* and *r*?

(*d*) Can you form any different tessellations with the remainder of your triangles? When you have a new pattern, record it either by pasting triangles in the correct positions in your exercise book or by pricking through the vertices of a tracing of your triangle on to a sheet of plain paper.

8 Figure 11 shows how a regular tessellation can be used to form more intricate designs. Try some for yourself.

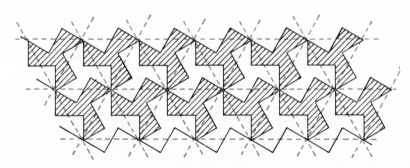

Fig. 11 (*a*)

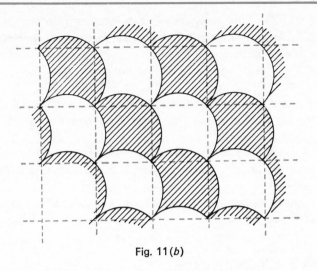

Fig. 11(*b*)

2. SYMMETRY

Figure 12 shows part of a tessellation of regular hexagons.

(*a*) Copy this tessellation on to isometric graph paper and make a second copy on tracing paper.

Prick a compass point through the vertex marked *A* and rotate the tracing paper until the two patterns are again superimposed.

Through what angle have you rotated the pattern? Is there more than one possible angle?

What is the order of rotational symmetry about the vertex *A*? (Imagine that the tessellation is extended to fill the whole plane.)

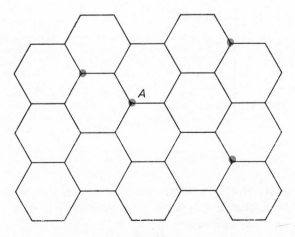

Fig. 12

(*b*) The red dots in Figure 12 mark centres of rotational symmetry of order 3. Can you find any other centres of rotational symmetry? State the order in each case.

(*c*) The tessellation also has line symmetry. How many lines of symmetry pass through the centre of each hexagon?

(*d*) Draw the regular tessellation of squares and trace the pattern. Use the tracing to find centres of rotational symmetry. State the order in each case.

How many lines of symmetry pass through the centre of each square? Are there any lines of symmetry which do not pass through the centre of a square?

(*e*) Describe the symmetries of the regular tessellation of equilateral triangles (see Figure 2).

Exercise B (Class projects)

1   Shapes made from squares joined edge to edge are sometimes called polyominoes.

Domino :   made from two squares.
Tromino :   made from three squares.
Tetromino :   made from four squares.
Pentomino :   made from five squares.

Fig. 13

There is just one domino.

Fig. 14

There are two trominoes. Any other arrangements of three squares can be rotated or turned over to look like one of these.

How many tetrominoes are there?

How many pentominoes?

Draw sketches to show that tessellations can be made from all the polyominoes with one, two, three, four or five squares.

The shapes made from 6 squares are called hexominoes. Tessellations can be formed from all of them. Draw some of these tessellations and colour them so that a shape does not have an edge in common with a shape of the same colour (see Figure 11).

Can you find a shape made from 7 squares with which you cannot form a tessellation?

2   Shapes made from equilateral triangles joined edge to edge are sometimes called polyiamonds.

Diamond: made from two equilateral triangles.
Triamond: made from three equilateral triangles.
Tetriamond: made from four equilateral triangles.
Pentiamond: made from five equilateral triangles.

How many triamonds, tetriamonds and pentiamonds are there? Can you form tessellations from all of these?

3   There are only 3 regular tessellations but other patterns can be formed from regular polygons when more than one kind are used. Use your cut-out polygons to find as many of these patterns as you can. Figure 15 shows two examples.

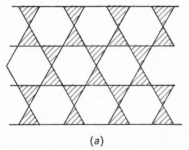
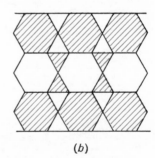

(a)   (b)

Fig. 15

When you find a pattern, record it. One attractive way of doing this is to cut the shapes from coloured gummed paper, stick them on to plain paper and display the finished patterns in the classroom.

When the shapes surrounding every vertex are in the same order, the tessellation is called semi-regular. Each vertex in Figure 15(a) is surrounded by hexagon, triangle, hexagon, triangle, in that order. In Figure 15(b), some vertices are like those in Figure 15(a); others are surrounded by hexagon, triangle, triangle, hexagon. The first pattern is semi-regular; the second is not. Sort your patterns into two sets:

21

those that are semi-regular and those that are not. There are eight semi-regular tessellations. Have you found all of them?

4   Make a collection of all the polyhedra which you have made. Which of them can be arranged to fill space?

5   Describe the symmetries of each of the eight semi-regular tessellations.

6   Design some tessellations with rotational symmetry of order 4. If possible, design a tessellation with rotational symmetry of order 4 only (that is, with no lines of symmetry).

Summary

Patterns which completely 'fill' the plane are called *tessellations*. A tessellation can be built from one basic unit, for example, a parallelogram. A tessellation can also be built from two or more basic units, for example, a square and a regular octagon.

A *regular tessellation* is a tessellation of regular polygons, all of one kind, and such that every vertex of the pattern is exactly like every other vertex. There are three regular tessellations: the pattern of squares on a sheet of graph paper, the pattern of equilateral triangles on isometric paper and the pattern of regular hexagons shown in Figure 12.

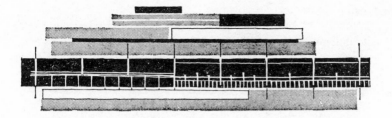

3. Decimals

1. MEASUREMENT

1.1 Units of length

Take *any* pencil and measure to see how many 'pencil-lengths' wide your desk is. Compare results. Did you find that everyone having the same sized desk as you, had the same result? If not, why not?

Can you think of a better way of comparing or measuring the widths of your desks?

How many centimetres wide is your desk? Did you get a whole number of centimetres for your answer? Compare results with anyone having the same sized desk as yourself. Even now, when everybody is using the *same unit of length* to measure with, you probably do not agree entirely as to the width of your desks. Why not?

1.2 Fractions of units

You have probably already found the need for fractions of a unit when trying to give fairly accurate measurements. What fraction of a unit did you use?

Figure 1 shows the measurement of the line segment *AB*. Each unit is divided into tenths. We could say that the length of *AB* is

(*a*) a bit more than 2 units;

or, to be more precise,

(*b*) just over $2\frac{3}{10}$ units.

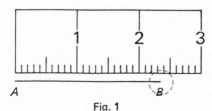

Fig. 1

Alternatively, we could say that the length of *AB* is

(*a*) 2 units (to the nearest unit) ;

or, to be more precise,

(*b*) $2\frac{3}{10}$ units (to the nearest tenth of a unit).

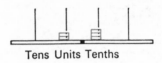

Tens Units Tenths

Fig. 2

Figure 2 shows the number $2\frac{3}{10}$ represented on an abacus. We could write this as $2 \cdot 3_{\text{ten}}$, using a fraction point. What would one disc on the unlabelled spike represent?

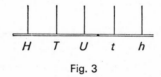

H   T   U   t   h

Fig. 3

Figure 3 shows an abacus designed for use in decimal arithmetic. What do the letters *H, T, U, t* and *h* stand for?

When we are working in base ten, we usually refer to the 'fraction point' as the 'decimal point'. We usually leave out the word ten, writing $2 \cdot 3_{\text{ten}}$ as $2 \cdot 3$.

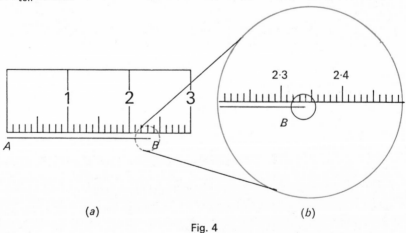

(*a*)   (*b*)

Fig. 4

Figure 4 shows us how to give the length of the line segment *AB* more accurately than before. Figure 4 (*b*) is an enlargement of the end of the segment near *B*. Each tenth of a unit has been divided into ten smaller equal parts (hundredths of a unit). We can now say that the length of *AB* is

(*c*) 2·34 units (to the nearest hundredth of a unit).

Can we say that *AB* is *exactly* 2·34 units long? Suppose you were to look at the black circled part, through a microscope. You might find that *AB* was just a little more than or just a little less than 2·34 units.

When we measure any length, we *compare* it with a fixed *unit*. It is because we are only *comparing* and not *counting* that we cannot talk about an *exact* length. Even if we divided the unit into smaller parts, we could not be certain that we had made an exact comparison.

Whenever we state a measure, which is a number, we must follow it with the unit we have used for comparison.

Exercise A

Which of the following activities involve measurement and which require only counting? In which is it possible to give an exact answer?

1 (*a*) Finding the number of pupils in your school;
  (*b*) finding the distance between your home and school;
  (*c*) finding your own weight;
  (*d*) finding the number of steps to the top of St Paul's Cathedral;
  (*e*) finding the temperature of a saucepan of milk;
  (*f*) finding the number of peas in a packet of frozen peas;
  (*g*) finding the time you take to walk one kilometre;
  (*h*) finding the number of words on a page of a book;
  (*i*) finding your age at mid-day on January 1st of this year.

2 Write the following in number symbols using the decimal point when necessary. (Remember that when we write whole numbers we do not need to put in the decimal point, but its position *would be* immediately after the digit which represents the units.)

(*a*) Five units;   (*b*) three hundredths;
(*c*) three hundreds;   (*d*) two and one tenth;
(*e*) six and five hundredths;   (*f*) seven hundreds and six tenths.

3 What does the 4 stand for in each of these numbers?

(*a*) 41·6;   (*b*) 1004;   (*c*) 6·4;
(*d*) 4321;   (*e*) 0·04.

4 Draw an abacus like the one in Figure 3 to represent each of the following 'decimal numbers':

(a) $7\frac{3}{10}$; (b) $24\frac{7}{10}$; (c) $123\frac{4}{10}$;
(d) 6·8; (e) 314·25; (f) 62·08;
(g) $13\frac{23}{100}$; (h) $106\frac{37}{100}$; (i) 0·32.

5 Explain the difference between the following numbers. What does the nought tell you in each case?

(a) 62·01 and 62·1; (b) 38 and 380;
(c) 47·16 and 47·106; (d) 13 and 103.

6

?	Hundreds	Tens	Units	Tenths	Hundredths	?
5	2	0	0			
	5	2	0			
		5	2			

(a) What column headings would you give to the unlabelled columns?

(b) By completing the table, add three more numbers to the sequence 5200, 520, 52, ..., ..., ... What is the connection between each number and the next number to the right?

Draw six abaci, one under the other, and show one of these numbers on each. What is the connection between the discs on the spikes and the numbers in the columns?

Add three more numbers to the following sequences:

(c) 93000, 9300, 930, ..., ..., ...;

(d) 0·019, 0·19, 1·9, ..., ..., ...

What is the connection between each number and the next number to the right in (c) and (d)?

2. STANDARD UNITS OF LENGTH

The standard unit of length is the metre (m). Other units are often used but they are either multiples or decimal fractions of the metre.

For smaller objects, the centimetre (cm) is used, where 100 cm = 1 m. (There is another small unit, the millimetre (mm), where 1000 mm = 1 m.) For longer distances, the kilometre (km) is used, where 1 km = 1000 m.

$$1 \text{ km} = 1000 \text{ m,}$$

$$1 \text{ cm} = \frac{1}{100} \text{ m,}$$

$$1 \text{ mm} = \frac{1}{1000} \text{ m.}$$

Each unit can be expressed as a multiple or a decimal of the other. For example:

1 m	=	100 cm;	100 cm	= 1 m;
4 m	=	400 cm;	1 cm	= 0·01 m;
0·5 m	=	50 cm;	18 cm	= 0·18 m;
1·73 m	=	173 cm;	160 cm	= 1·60 m;
1 km	= 1000 m;		1000 m	= 1 km;
2 km	= 2000 m;		1 m	= 0·001 km;
1·6 km	= 1600 m;		97 m	= 0·097 km;
0·05 km	=	50 m;	365 m	= 0·365 km.

Exercise B

1 With what units of length would you choose to measure:

(a) the width of your classroom;

(b) the height of your classroom;

(c) your own height;

(d) the thickness of this book?

Now carry out these measurements. What practical difficulties did you find?

2 With what units of length would you choose to measure the following:

(a) the length of your garden;

(b) the distance from London to Glasgow;

(c) the length of a match;

(d) the thickness of a sheet of paper;

(e) the distance between Earth and Mars?

3 Measure the lengths of these line segments. Give each length:

(i) to the nearest centimetre;

(ii) to the nearest tenth of a centimetre.

(a) ——————   (b) ——————

(c) ——————   (d) ————

(e) ——   (f) ——————

Could you *by eye* estimate each length correct to the nearest centimetre?

4 Draw, as accurately as you can, line segments of the following lengths:

(a) 4 cm;   (b) 2·3 cm;   (c) 1·8 cm;

(d) 0·7 cm;   (e) 10·5 cm;   (f) 15·8 cm;

(g) 13·2 cm;   (h) 20·1 cm.

Will any of your line segments be exactly the length mentioned?

5 Which of the following statements would you criticize and why?

(a) I am exactly 1·52 m tall.

(b) There are exactly 100 cm in 1 m.

(c) I made this dress in 8 h 35 min.

(d) I measured this line segment with my ruler and it is exactly 3·8 cm long.

(e) There are exactly 1000 m in 1 km.

3. ADDITION AND SUBTRACTION SHOWN ON THE ABACUS

Addition and subtraction are easy when you are working with whole numbers, and they are just as easy when you are working with numbers which involve a decimal point.

Example 1

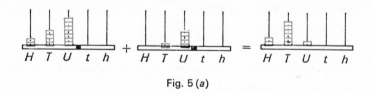

$$H \quad T \quad U \quad t \quad h \quad + \quad H \quad T \quad U \quad t \quad h \quad = \quad H \quad T \quad U \quad t \quad h$$

Fig. 5 (a)

This figure shows the addition

$$247 + 14 = 261 \quad \text{or} \quad \begin{array}{r} 247 \\ + \ 14 \\ \hline 261 \end{array}$$

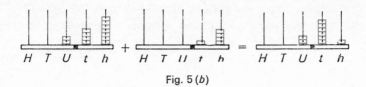

Fig. 5 (b)

This figure shows the addition

$$2\cdot47+0\cdot14 = 2\cdot61 \quad \text{or} \quad \begin{array}{r} 2\cdot47 \\ +\,0\cdot14 \\ \hline 2\cdot61 \end{array}$$

What do you notice about the two results?
What are: (i) 2470+140, (ii) 0·247+0·014?

Example 2

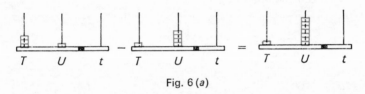

Fig. 6 (a)

This figure shows the subtraction

$$31 - 14 = 17 \quad \text{or} \quad \begin{array}{r} 31 \\ -\,14 \\ \hline 17 \end{array}$$

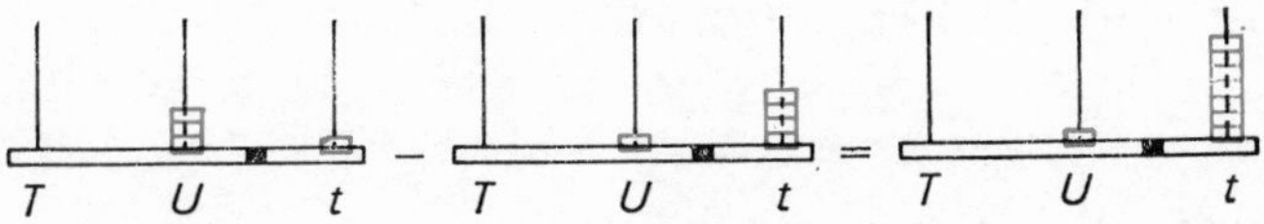

This figure shows the subtraction

$$3\cdot1 - 1\cdot4 = 1\cdot7 \quad \text{or} \quad \begin{array}{r} 3\cdot1 \\ -\,1\cdot4 \\ \hline 1\cdot7 \end{array}$$

Fig. 6 (b)

What do you notice about these results? What is $0.31-0.14$?

If we alter the place value of the digits but not their order, then basically the same calculation is involved. For example:

$$3100 \quad -1400 \quad = 1700$$
$$310 \quad - 140 \quad = 170$$
$$31 \quad - 14 \quad = 17$$
$$3.1 - \quad 1.4 \quad = \quad 1.7$$
$$0.31- \quad 0.14 = \quad 0.17$$

Exercise C

1   Draw a pair of diagrams to show the following calculations:

(a) $36.1+27.3$,   (b) $623-111$,
    $3.61+2.73$; $6.23-1.11$.

For each pair of calculations, what do you notice?

2   Work out the following:

(a) $\begin{array}{r} 4.91 \\ +3.68 \\ \hline \end{array}$

(b) $\begin{array}{r} 23.04 \\ +8.19 \\ \hline \end{array}$

(c) $\begin{array}{r} 104.3 \\ +0.12 \\ \hline \end{array}$

(d) $\begin{array}{r} 16.8 \\ -2.9 \\ \hline \end{array}$

(e) $\begin{array}{r} 3.87 \\ -0.08 \\ \hline \end{array}$

(f) $\begin{array}{r} 2.11 \\ -1.95 \\ \hline \end{array}$

3   Set out the following in the way shown in Question 2, then work them out.

(a) $2.9+0.11$;   (b) $3.64-0.91$;   (c) $20.07+104$;
(d) $34.36-17.82$;   (e) $81.6-1.92$;   (f) $10.1-0.08$;
(g) $1101-11.01$;   (h) $3.508-1.249$.

4. DECIMAL COINAGE

We have just seen that it is not difficult to add and subtract decimal numbers. This is one of the reasons why most countries use a decimal coinage system. Let us look at the system that has the 'pound' as the basic unit. This is divided into 100 smaller units called 'new pence' (p) so that:

$$100p = £1$$

and
$$1p = £\tfrac{1}{100} = £0{\cdot}01.$$

Any number of new pence can be expressed as a decimal of a pound. For example:

$$2p = £0{\cdot}02;$$
$$3p = £0{\cdot}03;$$
$$10p = £0{\cdot}10;$$
$$25p = £0{\cdot}25;$$
$$70p = £0{\cdot}70;$$
$$125p = £1{\cdot}25.$$

Notice that when *less than* 100p is expressed in pounds, a zero is always written before the decimal point. If we did not do this, we might confuse £·25 with £25.

Notice also that when stating parts of a pound, a digit is shown in *both* of the first two decimal places. £2·50 should never be written as £2·5, for this might be taken as £2 with only 5p, instead of 50p.

Exercise D

Work out the following:

1. (a)
$$\begin{array}{r} 17{\cdot}1 \\ +\,92 \\ \hline \end{array}$$

(b)
$$\begin{array}{r} 83{\cdot}2 \\ -\,51{\cdot}1 \\ \hline \end{array}$$

(c)
$$\begin{array}{r} 146{\cdot}1 \\ -\,23{\cdot}4 \\ \hline \end{array}$$

(d)
$$\begin{array}{r} 0{\cdot}761 \\ -\,0{\cdot}026 \\ \hline \end{array}$$

2. (a)
£
$$\begin{array}{r} 70{\cdot}93 \\ +\,81{\cdot}38 \\ \hline \end{array}$$

(b)
£
$$\begin{array}{r} 2{\cdot}67 \\ -\,1{\cdot}48 \\ \hline \end{array}$$

(c)
£
$$\begin{array}{r} 3{\cdot}42 \\ -\,1{\cdot}67 \\ \hline \end{array}$$

(d)
£
$$\begin{array}{r} 1{\cdot}31 \\ -\,0{\cdot}88 \\ \hline \end{array}$$

3   2·47 + 3·88 − 1·72.

4   £8·17 + £80·19 − £4·29.

5   Use your answers to Question 1 to *write down* the answers to the following:

(a) $+\begin{array}{r} 1·71 \\ 9·2 \end{array}$ (b) $-\begin{array}{r} 832 \\ 511 \end{array}$ (c) $-\begin{array}{r} 1·461 \\ 0·234 \end{array}$ (d) $-\begin{array}{r} 761 \\ 26 \end{array}$

6   The United States of America has a decimal coinage system based on the 'dollar' ($) which is divided into 100 smaller units called cents (c). European countries have similar systems based on a 'franc' 'mark', etc., which are divided into 100 smaller units.
   Work out the following:

	$		$		Fr.		Fr.
(a)	$+\begin{array}{r} 108·70 \\ 92·83 \end{array}$	(b)	$-\begin{array}{r} 23·21 \\ 19·53 \end{array}$	(c)	$+\begin{array}{r} 1·66 \\ 99·71 \end{array}$	(d)	$-\begin{array}{r} 32·91 \\ 26·99 \end{array}$

5. ROUNDING OFF AND SIGNIFICANCE

5.1   Rounding off

Is the length of this page 23·43 cm to the nearest hundredth of a centimetre? Can you measure as accurately as this with your ruler?

An ordinary ruler is marked in tenths of centimetres or, sometimes, only in whole centimetres. In such cases, we can check that the page length is 23·4 cm to the nearest tenth or 23 cm to the nearest whole centimetre.

Thinking of 23·43 cm to the nearest hundredth, as 23·4 cm to the nearest tenth, or as 23 cm to the nearest unit, is called 'rounding off'.

A sum of £2 467 983 spent on some national scheme, might well be rounded off to the nearest million pounds as £2 000 000, just for convenient reference. What is this sum of money rounded off to the nearest (i) half million; (ii) thousand pounds?

The number of people in a crowded stadium one day, is 29 381. To make this easy to remember, it might be rounded off to the nearest thousand as 29 000. What would it be to the nearest ten thousand?

What is the length of the line segment *AB* in Figure 7 (i) to the nearest tenth of a unit, (ii) to the nearest unit?

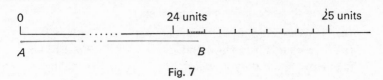

Fig. 7

When rounding off to the nearest tenth, 24·16 becomes 24·2, as the '6 hundredths' indicate that we are nearer 2 tenths than 1 tenth. In rounding off to the nearest unit, we have 24, as the '1 tenth' indicates that we are nearer 4 units than 5 units.

It is customary to round off a number such as 24·1<u>5</u>, 'upwards' as 24·2.

5.2 Significant figures

(*a*) Numbers are rounded off for various reasons: because of inaccurate instruments, for ease of reference and to make them easier to remember. We also round off so that we can concentrate upon the most important or *significant* digits. In the numbers

190·3   and   0·01903,

which digit is the most significant? Does this depend upon the size of the digit or upon its place value?

The most significant digits are always those whose *place value* is greatest, that is, those on the left. The '1' is more significant than the '9'. The '9' is more significant than the '3'.

The number of significant digits or 'figures' we choose, depends upon the circumstances. A distance of 17·5 km to a long distance runner in training might be rounded off to 18 km by a man who is walking for pleasure or to 20 km by a motorist. The runner is interested in 3 significant figures (we write this as '3 S.F.'), the walker in 2 S.F. and the motorist in 1 S.F.

A house is for sale at £3780. Write this number rounded off to 1 S.F. and again to 2 S.F. A rich man might well think in thousands of pounds. To him there is only one significant figure, the '4' in £4000. A poorer man might worry about the hundreds of pounds. To him there are two significant figures, the '3' and '8' in £3800.

Exercise E

1   Write down the following lengths rounded off to the nearest tenth of a unit:

(*a*) 7·13 m;   (*b*) 10·39 m;   (*c*) 22·22 m;
(*d*) 103·66 cm;   (*e*) 8·55 cm;   (*f*) 0·85 cm;
(*g*) 0·93 km;   (*h*) 0·99 km;   (*i*) 8·50 km.

2 Here are three questions and answers:

(*a*) 'How much did your new car cost?'   '£693·47'.
(*b*) 'How far is it to New York?'   '7283·14 km'.
(*c*) 'How much do you weigh?'   '49·37 kg'.

In each case, say why the answer is ridiculous and give a sensible answer.

To how many significant figures did you give your answers? Are you necessarily going to agree with your friends?

3 Write down the following numbers rounded off to (i) 1 S.F. and (ii) 2 S.F.:

(*a*) 142;   (*b*) 177;   (*c*) 949;   (*d*) £63·15;
(*e*) 12·14 km;   (*f*) 23·2 m;   (*g*) 15 km;   (*h*) £301;
(*i*) £7004;   (*j*) 1040 km;   (*k*) 1090 km;   (*l*) 1150 m.

4 To how many significant figures have the following measurements been given?

(*a*) 3 cm;   (*b*) 4·1 cm;   (*c*) 4·10 cm;   (*d*) 6·00 m;
(*e*) 105 km;   (*f*) 88·5 km;   (*g*) 7·13 km;   (*h*) 2·01 cm.

D 5 To how many significant figures are the following figures stated?

(*a*) The circumference of the earth is 40 000 000 metres.
(*b*) The height of Mount Everest is 8882 m.
(*c*) The population of the world in 1960 was 2 717 350 000.

D 6 (*a*) If you were timing a 100 m sprint to what accuracy would you want to be able to give the time? (To the nearest unit, or tenth, or hundredth...of a second?)

(*b*) If you are measuring an angle with a protractor, to what accuracy can you give your answer in degrees?

(*c*) To what accuracy can you weigh flour on ordinary kitchen scales?

(*d*) 'Her wage is about £16 per week.' Is it likely that the '£16' has been rounded off to the nearest unit?

(*e*) 'He is 12 years old and is already 130 cm tall.' Have these quantities been rounded off to the nearest unit?

(*f*) A pair of shoes is marked at £2·95. What is this rounded off to the nearest pound? Why are the extra 5p not added to the price?

Interlude

NUMBER NAMES

In this book, all the pages, chapters, sections, figures, questions and examples are numbered. As the numbers are always attached to the same pages, figures, etc., they can be used as *names* for the pages and figures. We refer to 'page 137' or to 'Figure 3'.

Write about things outside the school which you know are given number names. Explain why they are often more useful than word names. Can number names ever be combined, for example, by addition or subtraction?

Here are some suggestions that you can use to get you started:

House numbers. How are house numbers arranged along a street? Is the same arrangement always used? Do the two sides of a street ever get out of order?

Car numbers. Could all the numbers be replaced by letters? Does the order in which numbers are attached to cars matter?

Why are there numbers on some peoples' uniforms? (For example, those of bus conductors and policemen.)

Road numbers. Are there other ways of numbering roads? Are streets in a town numbered? Look at a map of the main roads in England. Can you see any order in the way the roads coming out of big cities are numbered?

Valuable manufactured articles. Very often things like bicycles, cameras, clocks and trains are numbered. What are the uses of these number names?

Have you a number name?

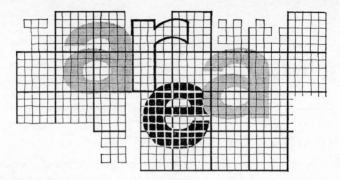

4. Area

1. COMPARISON OF AREA

Can you tell which of these two shapes is the larger?

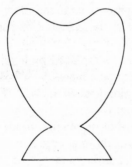

Fig. 1

If the shapes are nearly the same size, it is not easy to tell which is the larger just by looking at them. We need a way of *comparing* the areas. Discuss how you might do this.

You could, for example, see how many small coins of the same size you could fit inside each shape (see Figure 2). This *might* give you a rough guide. How?

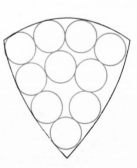

Fig. 2

36

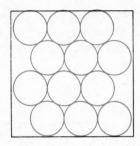 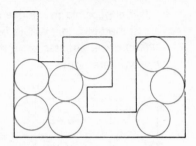

Fig. 3

There are two reasons, however, why the coin shown in Figure 2 was a particularly bad choice for the comparison of these two shapes. What are they?

Look at Figure 3. Count the number of coins fitted inside each shape. Which would you estimate to be the larger? How certain are you?

1.1 Tessellations and units of area

(*a*) In Chapter 3, we found that when comparing the widths of desks, it was necessary for everybody to use the same unit of length. (A 'pencil-length' unit is not much use when the pencils are different sizes.) In a similar way, when you compare the areas of two shapes everyone must use the same unit of area.

(*b*) The units of area must be the same size but they need not be the same shape though this is usually convenient. What would be the difficulty in comparing areas, if one shape was measured with circles and the other with triangles?

(*c*) The unit of area we used in Section 1 was a circle that was 9 mm across. However, we have seen that it was not a good choice. It would have been better to have chosen a shape that left no gaps.

For example, Figure 4 shows the shapes of Figure 1 filled with squares of the same size. At least the squares fit together more tightly.

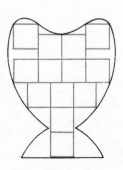 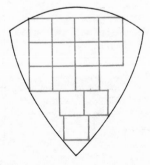

Fig. 4

Area

If it is possible to choose a shape to fit exactly into both the areas we are comparing, this would be better still. (See Figure 5.)

Count the squares to find which has the larger area. Are you certain that you are right?

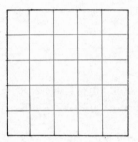 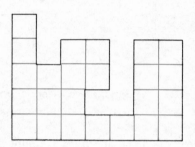

Fig. 5

Exercise A

1 Compare these pairs of shapes. Say which is the larger of each pair.

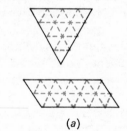 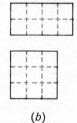 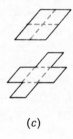

(a)   (b)   (c)

2 Count the square tiles to compare the areas of each pair of shapes.

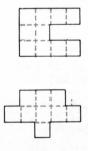 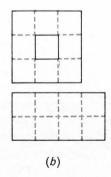 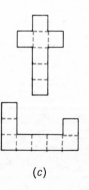

(a)   (b)   (c)

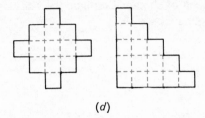

(*d*)

3 Count the triangular tiles to compare the areas of each pair of shapes.

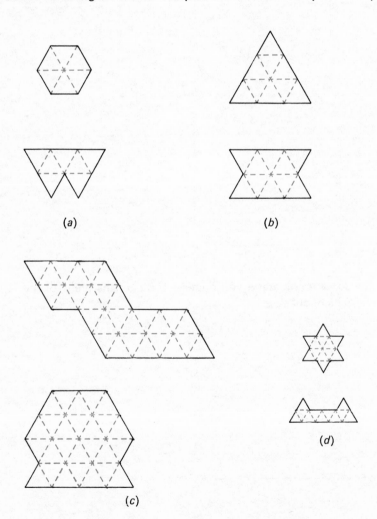

(*a*)   (*b*)

(*c*)   (*d*)

4 Trace each pair of shapes. Compare their sizes by filling them in with tiles of the given shape.

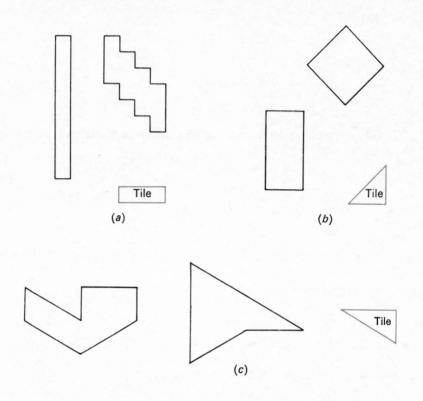

(a) (b)

(c)

5 Using any method you choose, compare the areas of the following pairs of shapes.

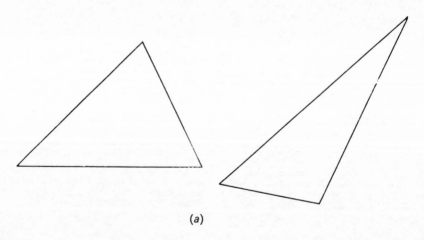

(a)

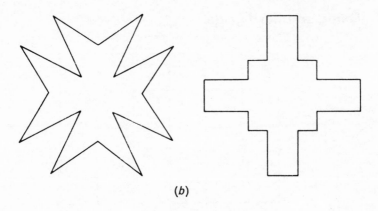

(b)

2. MEASUREMENT OF AREA

When we want to *compare* the areas of two figures, we choose the most convenient unit of area. But we often need to *measure* and describe the area of one figure. To do this, we compare it with some fixed standard unit of area which is familiar to everyone (just as we did for lengths). The *shape* of the standard unit of area can still be chosen for our own convenience. When we state that a certain area is 37 units we give no indication of the shape of the region.

Two common units of area are the square centimetre (cm²) and the square metre (m²). The following shapes each have an area of one square centimetre.

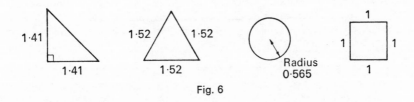

Fig. 6

You can see from the units of length associated with these areas that the square-shaped unit would be the easiest one to draw.

A square metre is roughly the area covered by 24 of these books.

Because it is a process of comparison with a standard unit, any measure of area can only be approximate. For greater accuracy we have to use fractions of the unit area and greater care in the comparison.

2.1 Using standard grids

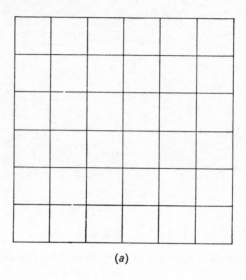

(a)

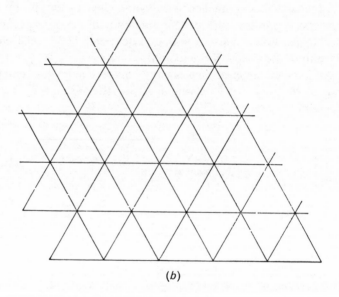

(b)

Fig. 7

The squares of Figure 7 (a) are one square centimetre in area. So are each of the equilateral triangles of Figure 7 (b).

To find the area of an irregular figure, it is convenient to use tracing paper. Either the outline of the figure can be traced and the tracing held over the top of the grid so that the squares can be counted, or the grid can be placed on tracing paper and held over the figure.

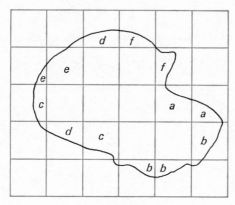

Fig. 8

Figure 8 shows a shape drawn over the square grid. It is possible to count and *estimate* its area from the figure.

How many complete centimetre squares are there?

The complete squares have area	7
Two parts marked *a*	1
Three parts marked *b*	1
Two parts marked *c*	1
Two parts marked *d*	1
Two parts marked *e*	1
Two parts marked *f* together with the small unlettered parts	1
	13 squares

Exercise B

1 Draw each of the following quadrilaterals on centimetre graph paper:

(a) (2, 0), (0, 2), (2, 4), (3, 2);

(b) (0, 1), (3, 1), (7, 5), (4, 5);

(c) (4, 0), (6, 1), (6, 7), (0, 4).

Find the area of each figure by counting squares.

2

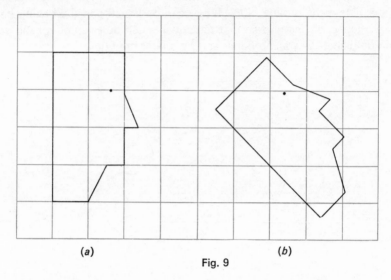

(a)   (b)

Fig. 9

The area of the polygonal man in Figure 9 (a) is approximately $7\frac{1}{2}$ cm². Another polygonal man is shown in Figure 9 (b). Has he the same area? Count squares to check your answer.

3 Draw a circle of radius 4 cm on graph paper and estimate the area enclosed.

Draw another circle with radius 2 cm. Would you expect the area of this circle to be half that of the first circle? Check your answer.

4 Use tracing paper and centimetre graph paper to compare the areas of the following pairs of English counties:

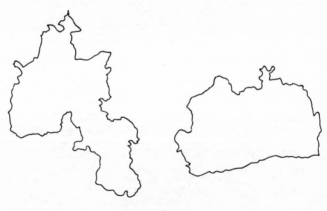

Fig. 10 (a)

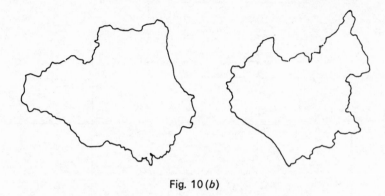

Fig. 10 (*b*)

Try to identify the counties. You can then check your answers from Whittaker's Almanac.

5 Use centimetre graph paper to discover the areas of irregular shapes of your own choice.

6 Take a length of string and knot it to form a loop. Arrange the loop to form different shapes. Have they all the same area? If not, what is the smallest area you can enclose? What shape encloses the largest area? What shape of triangle is the largest that can be made?

3. AREAS OF RECTANGLES

Look at the rectangle below.

Figure 11 (*a*) has been completely filled with 12 squares of side 1 cm. We say that its area is 12 cm².

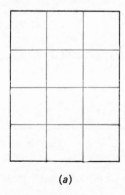

(*a*)

Fig. 11

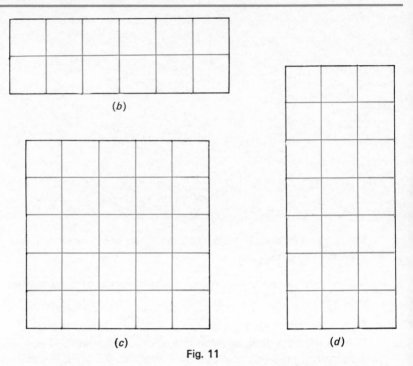

(b)

(c)   (d)

Fig. 11

Figures 11 (*b*), (*c*) and (*d*) have also been filled with centimetre squares. Count the squares to find the areas of these rectangles.

Look again at the dimensions (the width and length) of the rectangle. What is the connection between these and the area in each case?

(*a*) State the area (in cm²) of the rectangle in Figure 12 without first counting squares?

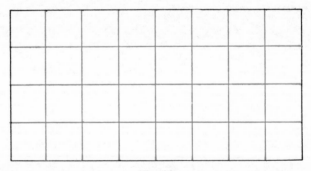

Fig. 12

(*b*) What is the area of a rectangle whose length and width are:

(i) 11 cm and 4 cm;   (ii) 6 cm and 8 cm?

(*c*) Measure the sides of the rectangle in Figure 13 to find its area.

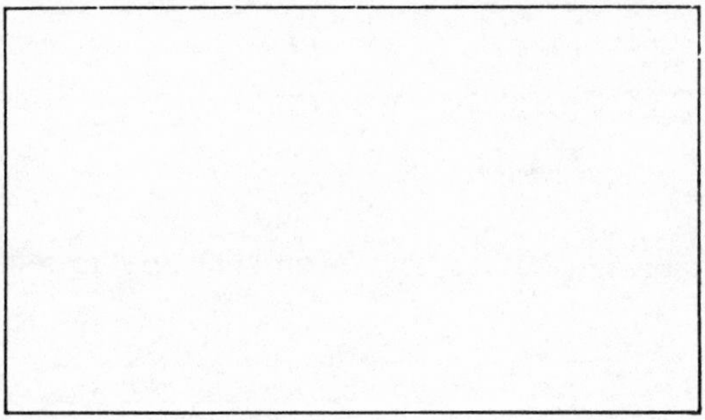

Fig. 13

(*d*) A rectangle has length *a* cm and width *b* cm (where *a* and *b* are counting numbers). What is its area?

Exercise C

1 (*a*) What is the area of a rectangle whose sides are:

(i) 3 cm and 4 cm;

(ii) 12 cm and 21 cm;

(iii) 2 km and 3 km?

(*b*) What are the areas of squares whose sides are:

(i) 10 cm;

(ii) 14 cm;

(iii) 30 cm?

(*c*) What is the length of rectangles where areas and widths are:

(i) 28 cm² and 2 cm;

(ii) 340 cm² and 17 cm;

(iii) 120 km² and 10 km?

(*d*) What is the length of a side of a square whose area is:

(i) 25 cm²;

(ii) 100 m²;

(iii) 1 km²?

2 Three rectangles have the following dimensions:

(*a*) 9 m and 6 m;

(*b*) 3 m and 17 m;

(*c*) 4 m and 14 m.

Which has the largest area and which the smallest?

3 What are the areas of the rectangles whose vertices are given by the following coordinates:

(a) (0, 0), (7, 0), (0, 3), (7, 3);

(b) (1, 2), (5, 2), (1, 6), (5, 6);

(c) (8 1), (13, 1), (8, 8), (13, 8)?

4 The following figures have been split up into rectangles. Find their areas.

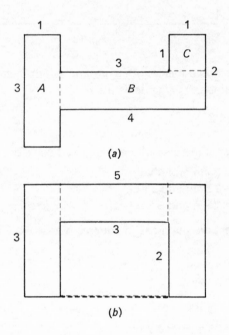

(a)

(b)

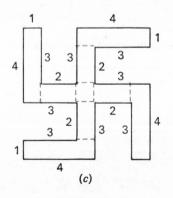

(c)

Fig. 14

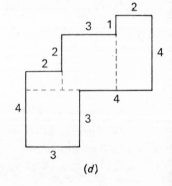

(d)

5 Split the following shapes into rectangles and find the area of each.

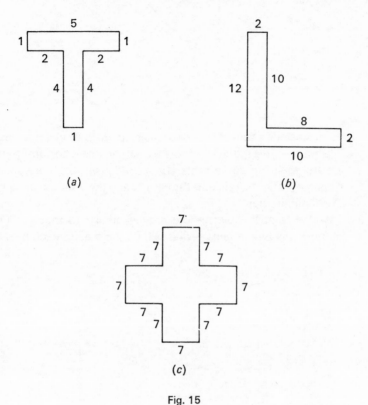

(a)

(b)

(c)

Fig. 15

6 How many tiles with dimensions 5 cm and 12 cm will be needed to fit a space whose dimensions are:

(a) 100 cm and 144 cm;

(b) 70 cm and 36 cm?

7 A rectangular floor of length 6 m is being covered by square tiles of side 20 cm. How many tiles will be needed to make a strip one tile wide the length of the room? If 720 tiles are needed altogether, what is the width of the room?

8 How many rectangles of area 20 cm^2 can be fitted into a rectangle of area 60 cm^2? Can this be done for any shape of rectangle? If not, give examples of rectangles of area 20 cm^2 which do not fit.

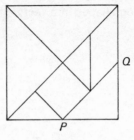

Fig. 16

An ancient Chinese puzzle consisted of cutting up a square into 7 pieces as in Figure 16, and then either trying to form them into a square again, or some other shape. Mark out a 5 cm square in the same way and, by pricking through, make the 7 pieces in card. (*P* and *Q* are middle points.)

Try to form the pieces into shapes similar to those in Figure 17 without any overlapping. What will be the area of each new shape?

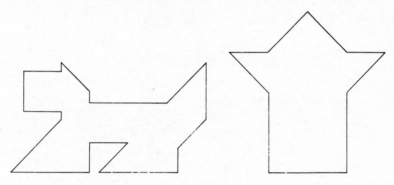

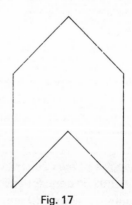

Fig. 17

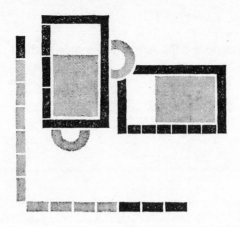

5. Comparison of fractions

1. REPRESENTING FRACTIONS

(a) In Book A, we showed the counting numbers as points on a line, as in Figure 1.

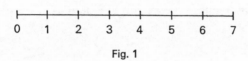

Fig. 1

Fractions are made up of two counting numbers? How can they be represented? How would *you* show $\frac{1}{4}$, $\frac{1}{2}$, $\frac{3}{4}$ and other fractions?

Perhaps you might decide to show them on two number lines, with the top number on one and the bottom number on the other. They could be joined with a line, like this

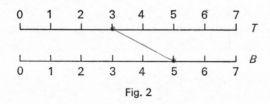

Fig. 2

What fraction do you think is shown in Figure 2?

Can you think of a better position for the *T* and *B* number·lines than having them one above the other?

Comparison of fractions

(*b*) Try drawing the *B* line at right-angles to the *T* line, meeting at 0, as in Figure 3.

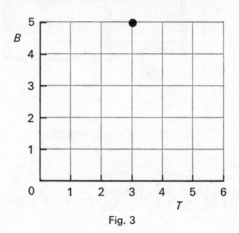

Fig. 3

Figure 3 shows $\frac{3}{5}$ again, but in a much neater way than is shown in Figure 2. Where do you remember seeing a different kind of number pair plotted in this way? We shall refer to this way of representing fractions as *graphing* the fractions.

(*c*) What fractions are shown in Figure 4?

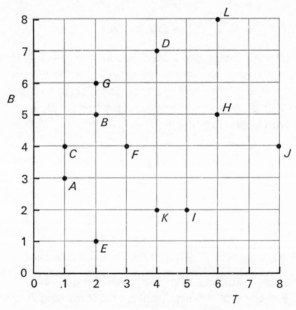

Fig. 4

(*d*) Draw the two number lines *T* and *B* as shown in Figure 4 and graph the following fractions:

(i) $\frac{2}{3}$, (ii) $\frac{5}{7}$, (iii) $\frac{4}{3}$, (iv) $\frac{5}{6}$, (v) $\frac{4}{5}$, (vi) $\frac{3}{2}$.

2. EQUIVALENT FRACTIONS

(*a*) Draw the lines *T* and *B* and graph the set of fractions:

$$\{\frac{3}{4}, \quad \frac{6}{8}, \quad \frac{9}{12}, \quad \frac{12}{16}\}.$$

What do you notice?
Now graph the set

$$\{\frac{1}{3}, \quad \frac{2}{6}, \quad \frac{3}{9}, \quad \frac{4}{12}\}.$$

What do you notice now?
Look carefully at the fractions in each set. What can you say about them?

(*b*) Draw five small circles of the same size. Shade $\frac{1}{2}$ of the first circle, $\frac{2}{4}$ of the second, $\frac{3}{6}$ of the third, $\frac{4}{8}$ of the fourth, and $\frac{5}{10}$ of the fifth circle. What do you notice about the shaded sections?
The fractions: $\frac{1}{2}, \frac{2}{4}, \frac{3}{6}, \frac{4}{8}, \frac{5}{10}$ are called 'equivalent' fractions.
Graph this set of equivalent fractions. What do you notice about the points? Did you expect this?

Exercise A

1 What fraction of each figure is shaded?

(*a*)  (*b*)  (*c*)

(*d*) 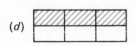 (*e*)  (*f*)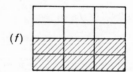

(*g*) 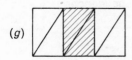 (*h*)

2 State some sets of equivalent fractions from the answers to Question 1.

3 What fraction of each of the following figures is shaded? Give your answers in two ways as two equivalent fractions.

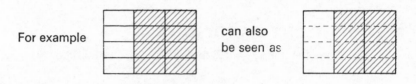

For example   can also be seen as

so $\frac{8}{12}$ and $\frac{2}{3}$ are equivalent fractions.

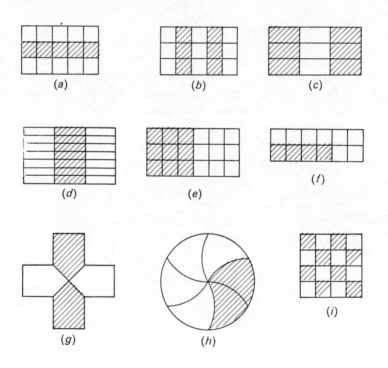

(a)   (b)   (c)

(d)   (e)   (f)

(g)   (h)   (i)

4 Trace each of the following figures, and by drawing more lines yourself, give two equivalent fractions for each of the shaded sections.

For example,
by drawing one more line   can be made into

so $\frac{1}{2}$ and $\frac{2}{4}$ are equivalent.

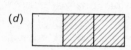 

5. Graph the sets of equivalent fractions you found in Question 2. What do you notice about each set of plotted points?

6. In each of the following sets there are three equivalent fractions. Graph the fractions, see which one does not lie on the line through the origin, and write down the odd man out.

(a) $\{\frac{1}{3}, \frac{2}{6}, \frac{3}{9}, \frac{8}{12}\}$; (b) $\{\frac{1}{4}, \frac{2}{8}, \frac{3}{12}, \frac{4}{14}\}$;

(c) $\{\frac{5}{10}, \frac{4}{8}, \frac{3}{6}, \frac{1}{4}\}$; (d) $\{\frac{2}{3}, \frac{4}{5}, \frac{6}{9}, \frac{8}{12}\}$.

7. Find the sets of equivalent fractions in Figure 4.

8.

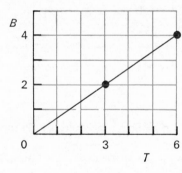

Fig. 5

The line passes through 0, so $\frac{3}{2}$ and $\frac{6}{4}$ are equivalent.

The line does not pass through 0, so $\frac{3}{2}$ and $\frac{5}{3}$ are *not* equivalent.

By graphing the following pairs of fractions as in Figure 5, see if they are equivalent to each other:

(a) $\frac{1}{2}, \frac{3}{4}$; (b) $\frac{3}{4}, \frac{9}{16}$; (c) $\frac{4}{7}, \frac{8}{14}$;

(d) $\frac{3}{4}, \frac{2}{3}$; (e) $\frac{3}{12}, \frac{1}{4}$; (f) $\frac{7}{21}, \frac{1}{4}$;

(g) $\frac{3}{8}, \frac{6}{16}$; (h) $\frac{4}{8}, \frac{1}{2}$.

2.1 Forming equivalent fractions

Graph the set of fractions

$$\left\{\tfrac{2}{3},\ \tfrac{4}{6},\ \tfrac{6}{9},\ \tfrac{8}{12},\ \tfrac{10}{15}\right\}.$$

Are the members of this set equivalent to each other?

How is the set of numbers on the tops of the fractions made up? Can you do the same for the set of numbers on the bottoms of the fractions? Can you write down some more members of this set of equivalent fractions? Graph the new fractions to see if they are correct.

In fact the tops of the fractions are multiples of two and the bottoms are multiples of three, like this

$$\left\{\frac{1\times2}{1\times3},\ \frac{2\times2}{2\times3},\ \frac{3\times2}{3\times3},\ \frac{4\times2}{4\times3},\ \frac{5\times2}{5\times3}\right\}.$$

So the next fraction is $\dfrac{6\times2}{6\times3}$, that is, $\dfrac{12}{18}$.

Write down some more members of the set

$$\left\{\tfrac{3}{4},\ \tfrac{6}{8},\ \tfrac{9}{12},\ \tfrac{12}{16},\ \ldots\right\}.$$

What multiples are being used for the top and bottom numbers of the fractions? Graph the fractions you have written down to see whether they are in fact equivalent.

Write down some more members of the set

$$\left\{\tfrac{2}{5},\ \tfrac{4}{10},\ \ldots\right\}.$$

What multiples are being used here?

Write down some members of the set of equivalent fractions

$$\left\{\tfrac{3}{7},\ \ldots\right\}.$$

Summary

Sets of equivalent fractions are made up by using multiples of the top and bottom numbers of the first fraction.

When a set of equivalent fractions is graphed, the points all lie on a straight line through the origin.

Exercise B

Write down a set of at least three fractions which are equivalent to each of the following fractions. Write them in two ways each time, so that, for example, $\tfrac{2}{5}$ gives

$$\left\{\frac{1\times2}{1\times5},\ \frac{2\times2}{2\times5},\ \frac{3\times2}{3\times5},\ \frac{4\times2}{4\times5}\ \ldots\right\}$$

or

$$\left\{\tfrac{2}{5},\ \tfrac{4}{10},\ \tfrac{6}{15},\ \tfrac{8}{20},\ \ldots\right\}.$$

Plot each set to see if you are correct.

1 (a) $\frac{3}{7}$;   (b) $\frac{4}{6}$;   (c) $\frac{3}{2}$;   (d) $\frac{5}{3}$.

2 (a) $\frac{1}{2}$;   (b) $\frac{5}{6}$;   (c) $\frac{4}{7}$;   (d) $\frac{7}{9}$.

3 (a) $\frac{4}{3}$;   (b) $\frac{5}{7}$.

3. COMPARING FRACTIONS

Which is bigger, $\frac{2}{4}$ or $\frac{1}{4}$? Draw a picture to show your answer.
Which is bigger, $\frac{2}{3}$ or $\frac{1}{3}$? Again draw a picture.
Which is bigger, $\frac{2}{6}$ or $\frac{3}{6}$? Do you need a picture in order to decide?
All these questions are easy to answer. But can you tell which is bigger, when the fractions are $\frac{5}{6}$ or $\frac{3}{4}$? Why is this question more difficult to answer than the previous ones?
The sets of fractions equivalent to $\frac{5}{6}$ and $\frac{3}{4}$ are written out below:

$$\left\{ \tfrac{5}{6},\ \left(\tfrac{10}{12}\right),\ \tfrac{15}{18},\ \tfrac{20}{24},\ \ldots \right\},$$

$$\left\{ \tfrac{3}{4},\ \tfrac{6}{8},\ \left(\tfrac{9}{12}\right),\ \tfrac{12}{16},\ \ldots \right\}.$$

It is clear that $\frac{10}{12} > \frac{9}{12}$, so it follows that $\frac{5}{6} > \frac{3}{4}$.

Exercise C

1 Write out the sets of fractions equivalent to each member of the following pairs. Pick out the two fractions with the same bottom number in order to see which fraction is bigger.

(a) $\frac{4}{6}$, $\frac{2}{3}$;   (b) $\frac{1}{2}$, $\frac{4}{7}$;   (c) $\frac{3}{4}$, $\frac{4}{6}$;   (d) $\frac{7}{8}$, $\frac{5}{6}$.

2 Graph your answers to Question 1 and see if the line of fractions equivalent to the bigger one is always nearer one of the axes. If it is, then this is another check on your working.

3 Write out the sets of fractions equivalent to each member of the following pairs, and plot sets of points to check that they are correct. Pick out the two fractions with the same bottom number in order to see which is bigger.
   Check to see if the line of fractions equivalent to the bigger one is closer to the T number line.

(a) $\frac{1}{3}$, $\frac{2}{5}$;   (b) $\frac{1}{4}$, $\frac{3}{8}$;   (c) $\frac{4}{6}$, $\frac{5}{7}$;   (d) $\frac{5}{8}$, $\frac{7}{12}$.

3.1 Calculating equivalent fractions

In Exercise C you were looking for the smallest number that appeared among the multiples of both the bottom numbers of the fractions you were comparing. If you could go through the multiples tables in your head, or even guess the smallest number appearing in both multiples tables, then of course this would be much quicker.

Exercise D

1 Copy and fill in the missing parts:

(a) $\dfrac{2}{3} = \dfrac{4 \times 2}{4 \times 3} = \dfrac{}{12}$;

(b) $\dfrac{3}{4} = \dfrac{5 \times 3}{5 \times 4} = \dfrac{}{20}$;

(c) $\dfrac{2}{5} = \dfrac{3 \times 2}{3 \times 5} = \dfrac{}{15}$;

(d) $\dfrac{3}{5} = \dfrac{}{4 \times 5} = \dfrac{}{20}$;

(e) $\dfrac{4}{7} = \dfrac{}{3 \times 7} = \dfrac{}{21}$;

(f) $\dfrac{5}{6} = \dfrac{\quad}{\quad} = \dfrac{}{24}$;

(g) $\dfrac{4}{9} = \dfrac{\quad}{\quad} = \dfrac{}{54}$;

(h) $\dfrac{3}{10} = \dfrac{\quad}{\quad} = \dfrac{}{60}$;

(i) $\dfrac{7}{11} = \dfrac{\quad}{\quad} = \dfrac{}{33}$;

(j) $\dfrac{5}{12} = \dfrac{\quad}{\quad} = \dfrac{}{60}$.

3.2 Graphing fractions to compare them

Example 1

Compare $\frac{2}{3}$ and $\frac{3}{4}$.

The smallest number appearing in both the multiples of three and multiples of four is 12; so

$$\tfrac{2}{3} = \tfrac{8}{12} \quad \text{and} \quad \tfrac{3}{4} = \tfrac{9}{12}.$$

Since $\quad \tfrac{9}{12} > \tfrac{8}{12}$, it follows that $\frac{3}{4} > \frac{2}{3}$.

Check:

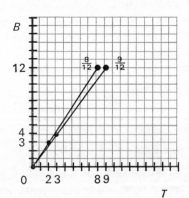

58

Example 2

Fractions with different bottom numbers can be added and subtracted using these ideas. Find the sum of $\frac{2}{3}$ and $\frac{1}{5}$.

The smallest number appearing in both the multiples of three and the multiples of five is 15.

$$\frac{2}{3} = \frac{10}{15} \quad \text{and} \quad \frac{1}{5} = \frac{3}{15}.$$

So

$$\frac{2}{3} + \frac{1}{5} = \frac{10}{15} + \frac{3}{15} = \frac{13}{15}.$$

Exercise E

1 Using the method of Example 1 compare:

(a) $\frac{3}{8}$ and $\frac{1}{3}$;   (b) $\frac{1}{4}$ and $\frac{2}{5}$;

(c) $\frac{2}{7}$ and $\frac{3}{10}$;   (d) $\frac{4}{5}$ and $\frac{7}{9}$;

(e) $\frac{5}{12}$ and $\frac{3}{10}$.

2 Using the method of Example 2, work out:

(a) $\frac{1}{2} + \frac{2}{3}$;   (b) $\frac{3}{4} + \frac{1}{6}$;

(c) $\frac{5}{6} - \frac{2}{3}$;   (d) $\frac{2}{3} - \frac{1}{4}$;

(e) $\frac{1}{2} + \frac{3}{8}$;   (f) $\frac{5}{6} + \frac{4}{9}$.

3 When dealing with mixed numbers, all that is necessary is to turn them into fractions. For example:

$$1\frac{1}{3} + 2\frac{1}{2},$$

$$1\frac{1}{3} = \frac{4}{3} = \frac{8}{6} \quad \text{and} \quad 2\frac{1}{2} = \frac{5}{2} = \frac{15}{6},$$

so

$$1\frac{1}{3} + 2\frac{1}{2} = \frac{8}{6} + \frac{15}{6} = \frac{23}{6} = 3\frac{5}{6}.$$

Now do the following:

(a) $1\frac{1}{2} + 1\frac{2}{3}$;   (b) $2\frac{1}{4} - 1\frac{2}{3}$;

(c) $1\frac{1}{6} - \frac{2}{3}$;   (d) $1\frac{5}{8} + \frac{2}{9}$;

(e) $2\frac{2}{3} + 1\frac{4}{5}$;   (f) $2\frac{5}{8} - 1\frac{1}{6}$.

3.3 The fraction number line

In Exercise C, you noticed that the larger the fraction the closer its line of equivalent fractions was to the T line. Let us look into this a little more closely.

Comparison of fractions

In Figure 6 the sets of equivalent fractions have been drawn for $\frac{1}{2}, \frac{1}{1}, \frac{2}{1}, \frac{3}{1}, \frac{4}{1}, \frac{5}{1}$. Where do these lines meet the line R?

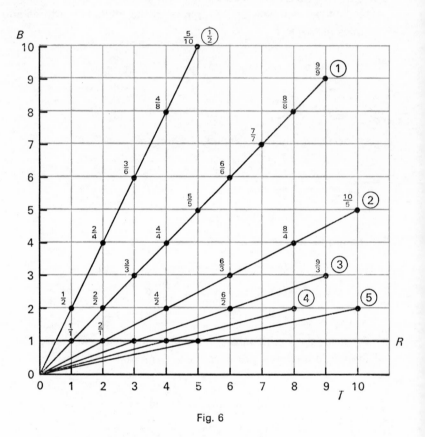

Fig. 6

In Figure 7, we have enlarged part of Figure 6 to show some more of the equivalent fraction lines that can be drawn. Look carefully at the places where they meet the line R. Why do you think that the line R can be thought of as the number line for fractions?

Make as large a drawing as you can and see how many fractions you can show on the number line R. Why can't you show any more? Are there any more fractions to graph?

How many fractions do you think there are on the number line? Does the complete set of fractions entirely cover the number line, or are there any gaps left?

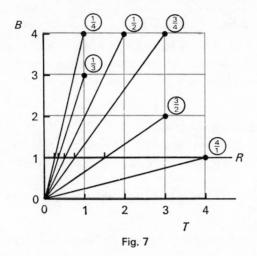

Fig. 7

What fractions are graphed in Figure 8? Now take a ruler, place it along the *B* line and turn it slowly about (0, 0) in a clockwise direction. As the ruler turns, it will uncover fractions in order of size, smallest first. Why?

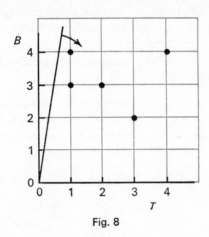

Fig. 8

Exercise F

1   Look back at Figure 4 and with the help of a ruler, write down all the fractions shown there, in order of size, smallest first. What do you notice about the fractions *A* and *G*? Why does this happen? Are there any more like this in the figure?

2   Arrange the following sets of fractions in order of size:

(*a*) $\frac{1}{4}$, $\frac{1}{6}$, $\frac{2}{9}$;

(*b*) $\frac{3}{5}$, $\frac{4}{7}$, $\frac{2}{3}$;

(*c*) $\frac{2}{3}$, $\frac{6}{7}$, $\frac{5}{6}$, $\frac{3}{4}$;

(*d*) $\frac{5}{11}$, $\frac{4}{9}$, $\frac{3}{7}$, $\frac{5}{8}$, $\frac{7}{10}$.

4. FAREY SEQUENCES

The Farey sequence of fractions of order 4 is the set of all simplified fractions less than one, whose bottom numbers are 4 or less, arranged in order of size. The members of this set are

$$\tfrac{1}{2}, \ \tfrac{1}{3}, \ \tfrac{2}{3}, \ \tfrac{1}{4}, \ \tfrac{3}{4}.$$

What has happened to $\tfrac{2}{4}$?

Graph the fractions, and with the help of a ruler arrange them in size, smallest first. Now find the Farey sequences of order 5 and 6 in the same way.

Exercise G

1 Write down the Farey sequence of order 7. Consider any three consecutive members. Find out how to combine the two outer ones to form the middle one. Check that the same rule applies to all triples (that is, sets of 3 consecutive numbers).

2 Consider any pair of consecutive members of the Farey sequence of order 4. Multiply the top number of the second by the bottom number of the first. Multiply the top number of the first by the bottom number of the second. Subtract your answers. Repeat this for another pair. What do you find? Check to see whether this is true in Farey sequences of order 5, 6 and 7.

*3 Find the number of members in the Farey sequences of orders 3, 4 and 5. Is there a general rule? Estimate the number for the sequence of order 6 and check it. Now check the number for the Farey sequence of order 7 which you obtained in Question 2. Explain what you find.

*4 Three consecutive members of a Farey sequence are

$$\ldots, \ \tfrac{1}{3}, \ \tfrac{3}{8}, \ \tfrac{2}{5}, \ \ldots.$$

Find the next member, bearing in mind your answers to Questions 1 and 2.

Revision exercises

1 Complete the fraction $\frac{?}{24}$ which is equivalent to $\frac{1}{3}$.

2 What is the perimeter of a regular hexagon of side 9 m?

3 Calculate:

(a) $\begin{array}{r} 23\cdot4 \\ +\ 17\cdot7 \\ \hline \\ \hline \end{array}$ (b) $\begin{array}{r} 149\cdot2 \\ -\ 99\cdot1 \\ \hline \\ \hline \end{array}$

4 What is the area of a rectangle of length $5\frac{1}{2}$ cm and width 4 cm?

5 Which of the following figures tessellate:

(a) regular hexagon;   (b) right-angled triangle;
(c) pentagon;   (d) quadrilateral;
(e) decagon?

6 Arrange in order of size, smallest first:

$$\frac{2}{3},\ \frac{3}{5},\ \frac{1}{4},\ \frac{5}{6},\ \frac{1}{2}.$$

Quick quiz, no. 2

1 A book costs £1·23. How much would 4 books cost?

2 Round off 337·52 to 2 significant figures.

3 If $A = \{$quadrilaterals$\}$ and $B = \{$regular polygons$\}$, what is $A \cap B$?

4 What is the area of a square whose perimeter is 8 cm?

5 List the subsets of $\{2, 3, 5, 7\}$ which have just two members.

6 Are the following true or false?

(a) $\frac{5}{8} > \frac{4}{7}$;   ($b$) $\frac{5}{6} < \frac{9}{11}$;   ($c$) $\frac{2}{3} + \frac{3}{4} = \frac{17}{12}$.

Revision exercises

Exercise A

1 State whether or not you would need to count accurately if you were:

(*a*) a bank clerk counting out £5 notes to a customer;

(*b*) a newspaper reporter wanting to give the size of the crowd at a football match;

(*c*) a scorer counting up the runs in an innings;

(*d*) a builder deciding how many bricks would be needed to build a block of flats;

(*e*) a driver reversing out of a garage who was told 'The road will be clear after the third car'.

2 Calculate the angles marked *p, q* and *r* (see Figure 1).

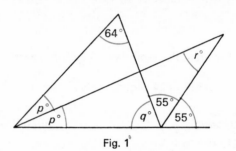

Fig. 1

3 A certain crossword composer always makes his diagrams with rotational symmetry of order 4. He has finished blacking in the squares of the top left-hand quarter of the diagram. Copy and complete Figure 2. How many 'across' clues will he have to invent? How many 'down'?

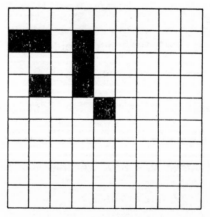

Fig. 2

4 Complete the following tables. They state:

(i) the length of each given line segment;

(ii) an expression for any length of the sequence in terms of n. (n is any member of the set of counting numbers.)

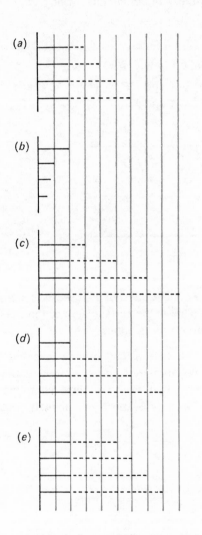

	Line	Length
(a)	1	$2+1$
	2	$2+2$
	3	$2+$
	4	$2+$
	n	$2+n$
(b)	1	$2 \div 1$
	2	$2 \div$
	3	$2 \div 3$
	4	$2 \div$
	n	$2 \div$
(c)	1	$2+1$
	2	$2+3$
	3	$2+$
	4	$2+$
	n	$2+$
(d)	1	2
	2	2×2
	3	2
	4	2
	n	2
(e)	1	2
	2	2
	3	$2+5$
	4	2
	n	2

5 Is it possible to make a tessellation using any shaped triangle as a basic motif?

How many different shaped quadrilaterals can you make by joining edge to edge:

(a) 2 identical equilateral triangles;

(*b*) 2 identical isosceles triangles;

(*c*) 2 identical scalene triangles (scalene triangles are triangles which have no two sides of the same length)?

Make sketches of your results. Would it be impossible to make a tessellation from any one of these quadrilaterals? If not, why not?

Exercise B

1   In Figure 3, what is the relation between:

(*a*) *AX* and *AD*;   (*b*) *AX* and *DC*;   (*c*) ∠*ADC* and ∠*DXC*;

(*d*) ∠*XDC* and ∠*DXC*;   (*e*) *DX* and *XC*?

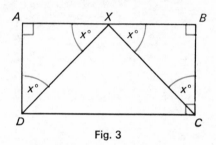

Fig. 3

2   Draw accurately a net for the construction of a closed box 6 cm long, $4\frac{1}{2}$ cm wide and 3 cm high. What is the surface area of the outside of the box? What is the total length of its edges?

3   Make three copies of Figure 4. In the first, outline in colour those shapes which have rotational symmetry of order exactly 2. Mark the centres of rotation. On the other two copies, outline the shapes with rotational symmetry of order exactly 3 and 6 respectively. Mark the centres of rotation.

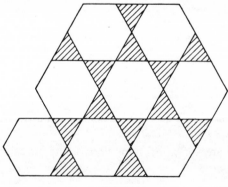

Fig. 4

4   Add together 3·87, 0·2485, 0·083 and 370.
Now write down your answer

   (*a*) correct to 2 significant figures, and

   (*b*) correct to 2 decimal places.

5   Make a drawing of two triangles whose sides intersect at

   (*a*) one point;   (*b*) two points;   (*c*) three points;

   (*d*) four points;   (*e*) five points;

   (*f*) six points;   (*g*) no points.

What is the greatest number of points at which the sides of 2 triangles can intersect? What is the greatest number of points at which the sides of two quadrilaterals can intersect?

What is the greatest number of points at which the sides of two hexagons can intersect?

What is the greatest number of points at which the sides of two *n*-sided figures can intersect?

6. Angle

1. FIXING A POSITION

A playground conversation (John and Malcolm are talking).

J.   'There you are, that's the boy who won the cross-country last year.'

M.   'Where?'

J.   'Over there, he's the one with the dark hair.'

M.   'I can see lots of boys with dark hair.'

J.   'Well you see the gate, don't you?'

M.   'Yes.'

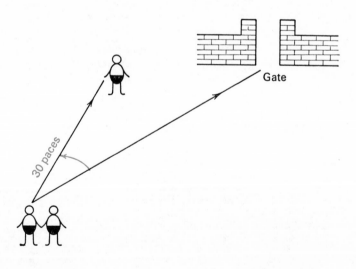

Gate

30 paces

J. 'Well now turn a little to your left, and you will see that he is about 30 paces away from us.'

M. 'The boy looking down now?'

J. 'Yes, that's him.'

This method of fixing a position depends on naming a landmark first (the gate), then talking of a turn and a distance. It works quite well over a short distance but is not very accurate. Why not?

2. THE CLOCK-RAY METHOD

A useful way of fixing a position, which has been developed in the Army, uses a clockface to indicate the required direction.

Imagine that you are standing at the centre of a clock which can be turned round so that 12 o'clock is in the direction of the landmark. You can then refer to the amount of turn needed to face the object you are talking about by the hours on the clockface. For example:

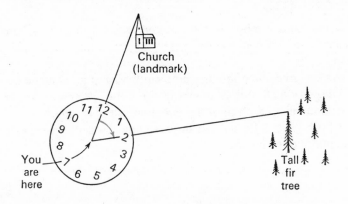

1 Turn the clock round so that 12 faces the landmark.

2 Give the hour which points to the object you are concerned with. In this case you would say to your friend:

'From the Church Steeple, 2 o'clock, Tall Fir Tree.'

Exercise A

Trace the drawing at the top of the next page into your exercise book. Take the top of the church steeple as 12 o'clock. Draw a clockface and give instructions to find all the other objects.

If one centimetre on this paper represents one hundred metres on the actual ground, say how far away from each object you are.

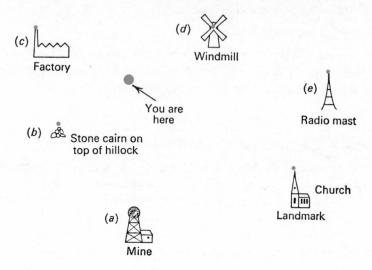

(c) Factory

(d) Windmill

(e) Radio mast

You are here

(b) Stone cairn on top of hillock

Church Landmark

(a) Mine

3. BEARINGS

The clock-ray method is still not very good. It might be hard to find a landmark and it might be necessary to give a more accurate measure of turn.

We can overcome the first problem by using a magnetic compass, the needle of which always points to the north. We can then let the north direction take the place of the direction of the landmark.

The second difficulty can be overcome by using degrees to measure the turn. For example:

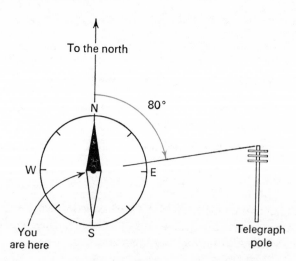

To the north

N

80°

W

E

You are here

S

Telegraph pole

In this case you would say to your friend, 'Bearing 080 degrees, telegraph pole.'

BEARINGS:
ALWAYS START FROM NORTH;
ALWAYS TURN CLOCKWISE

Exercise B

1   Use your protractor to measure the bearings of objects at points *A*, *B*, *C* and *D*, if you are standing at *O*.

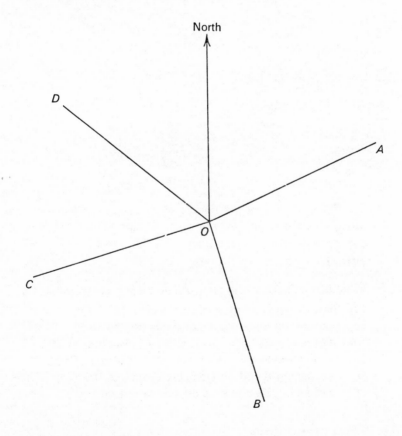

2   What is the bearing of:

   (*a*) north-east;   (*b*) south-east;   (*c*) north-west?

3 Trace the next drawing into your exercise book. Draw a straight line between your position and the red dot on each object, and give its bearing.

Take the scale to be one centimetre to one hundred metres, and say how far away from each object you are.

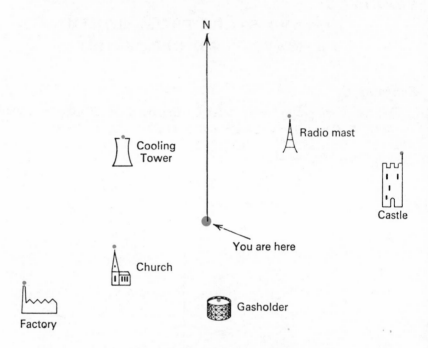

4 Start at a point near the middle of the page and draw a north line straight up the page. Draw lines to indicate the following bearings:

(a) 025°;   (b) 143°;   (c) 235°;
(d) 270°;   (e) 305°.

5 What is the final bearing after obeying each of the following?

(a) Start facing NE and do a clockwise turn of 50°.
(b) Start facing E and do a clockwise turn of 65°.
(c) Start facing SW and do an anticlockwise turn of 45°.
(d) Start facing W and do an anticlockwise turn of 40°.
(e) Start facing S and do a clockwise turn of 100°.
(f) Start facing SE and do a clockwise turn of 140°.

3.1 Plotting a course

Think of a ship about to leave this harbour and sail to the river mouth opposite.

The pilot would first look at the compass to find out where north was, and then note the bearing needed to clear the harbour mouth, in this case 070°.

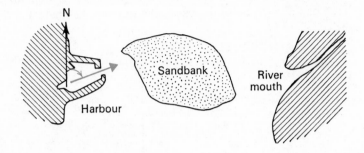

The ship would then sail on a bearing of 070° until it was outside the harbour. To miss the sandbank, the pilot would again find north and change to a bearing of 135°.

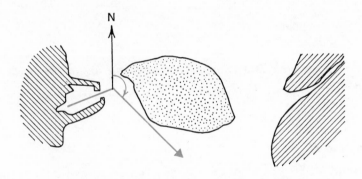

When clear of the sandbank, north would be found once again and a final bearing of 063° would be taken to the river mouth.

Note that this is only one of many possible courses.

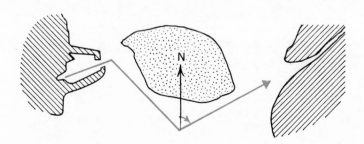

Angle

Example 1

An aircraft flies on a bearing of 055° for 500 km, and then changes course to a bearing of 120° and flies on this new course for 350 km.

Take one centimetre to represent one hundred kilometres and plot this course.

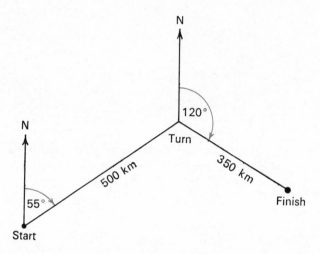

Whenever there is a change of course, put in another north direction arrow.

Exercise C

REMEMBER—Bearings are always taken as clockwise from north.

1 Describe each of these courses. Take the scale to be one centimetre to one hundred kilometres, and north straight up the page.

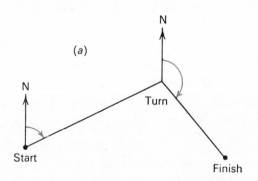

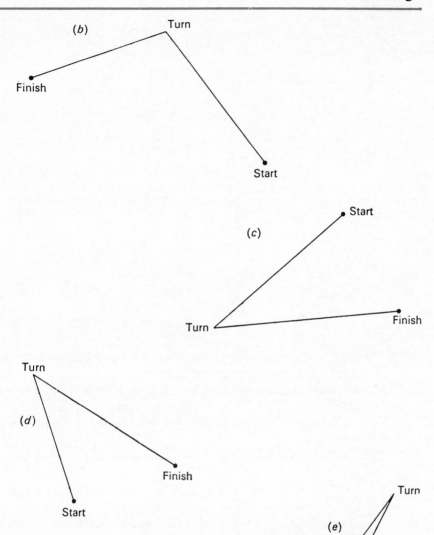

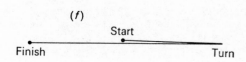

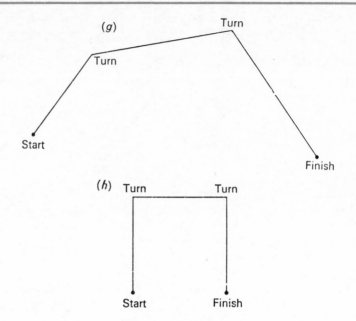

(g) Turn

Turn

Start

Finish

(h) Turn   Turn

Start   Finish

2 Plot the following courses using a scale of one centimetre to one hundred kilometres. Use squared paper.

(*a*) 550 km on a bearing of 070° followed by 400 km on a bearing of 150°.

(*b*) 340 km on a bearing of 300° followed by 600 km on a bearing of 045°.

(*c*) 320 km on a bearing of 210° followed by 340 km on a bearing of 170°.

(*d*) 350 km on a bearing of 035° followed by 490 km on a bearing of 100° followed by 570 km on a bearing of 075°.

(*e*) 500 km on a bearing of 030° followed by 500 km on a bearing of 150° followed by 500 km on a bearing of 270°.

3 Give the instructions for flying an aircraft round a square of side 100 kilometres. Start by flying due north.

4 If you are standing at *A*, what is the bearing of *B*? Can you answer this without using a protractor?

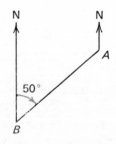

N   N

A

50°

B

5 What is the bearing of *P* from *Q*?

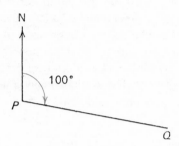

6 The bearing of a town *A* from a town *B* is 120°. What is the bearing of town *B* from town *A*?

7 A ship leaves port and sails for 20 km on a bearing of 080°; it then alters course to a bearing of 200° and sails for a further 15 km. Make a scale drawing of the complete track, and state the distance and bearing of the ship from the port.

8 A ship leaves port on a bearing of 060°. After 40 km it alters course to a bearing of 110° which it keeps for 50 km. By means of a scale drawing find the new position of the ship. What are its distance and bearing from the port?

9 Two planes leave an airport at the same time. One flies on a bearing of 330° at 800 km/h, while the other flies due east at 1200 km/h. Draw one diagram to show their positions and distances apart after:

(a) $\frac{1}{4}$ hour;   (b) $\frac{1}{2}$ hour;   (c) $\frac{3}{4}$ hour;   (d) 1 hour.

10 From the top of a hill three church spires can be seen.
The first, *A*, is 6 km away on a bearing of 330°; the second, *B*, is 4 km away on a bearing of 070°; and the third, *C*, is 2 km due south.
Draw a plan of the positions of the spires using a scale of 1 cm to 1 km.

(a) Measure the distances:

(i) *A* to *B*,   (ii) *B* to *C*,   (iii) *C* to *A*.

(b) What are the bearings of:

(i) *A* from *B*,   (ii) *B* from *C*,   (iii) *C* from *A*?

4. RADAR

Many of you will have seen a rotating aerial on ships or at ports and aerodromes. These are *radar* aerials. Radar is used to 'see' objects that are far away or which are hidden in mist or cloud. A signal like a radio or light wave is sent out from the aerial. It bounces off any object it meets, is picked up again by the aerial and appears on a *radar screen* in the form of a bright spot of light. The actual screen is like a television set except that it has angles and concentric circles marked on it.

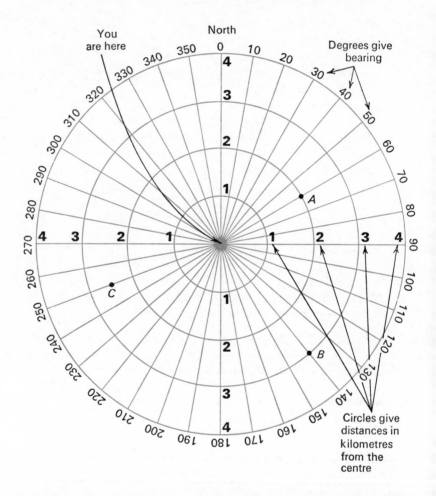

Imagine that you are the centre of the screen which represents a bird's-eye-view of the whole area around you. A point of light appearing on the screen will correspond to an object on the ground and you can immediately read off its distance and bearing. For example:

A is 2 km on a bearing of 060°;

B is 3 km on a bearing of 140°;

C is 2·5 km on a bearing of 250°.

We could write *A* as (2, 060) and remember that the first number stands for kilometres and the second number for degrees. This would save a lot of time and space if we had several positions to record.

How would you write the positions of *B* and *C* in this short way?

Exercise D

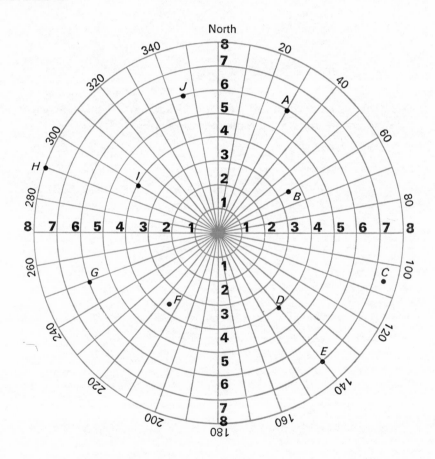

1 Use the shorthand method to give the distance and bearing of each of the points *A* to *J* on the radar screen above.

2 Trace this diagram of a harbour, and draw a radar screen centred on the Harbour master's office. Use concentric circles so that every centimetre represents 1 kilometre. Give the distance and bearing of all the points mentioned.

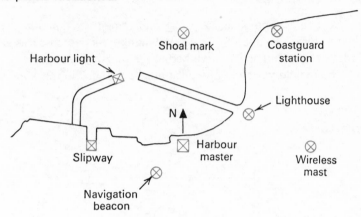

3 Draw a radar screen with eight circles, using 0·5 cm to represent each kilometre, and on it put the following points:

(a) (4, 025); (b) (6½, 070); (c) (2, 105);

(d) (8, 150); (e) (8, 215); (f) (5, 260);

(g) (7½, 260); (h) (1, 300); (i) (3, 343).

7. Relations

1. FAMILY RELATIONSHIPS

Figure 1 is a Family Tree. Why is it called a tree? This one tells you how a group of 15 people are related to one another. What does ' = ' mean? Does it make any difference if the first name is a man's or a woman's? What do the vertical lines mean? What do the horizontal lines indicate?

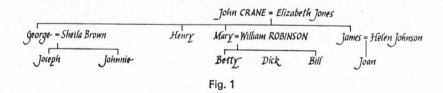

John CRANE = Elizabeth Jones

George = Sheila Brown   Henry   Mary = William ROBINSON   James = Helen Johnson

Joseph   Johnnie   Betty   Dick   Bill   Joan

Fig. 1

Exercise A

1   How many children have John and Elizabeth?

2   How many grandchildren have they?

3   How many children call Henry 'Uncle'?

4   How many nephews has he?

5   What is Johnnie's surname?

6   Write down the full names of everyone who has a brother.

7   How many different relationships are represented in this family?

1.1 Arrow diagrams

Figure 2 shows all the children in the family. What is the relationship between Joseph and Johnnie? Arrows can be drawn to indicate this relationship.

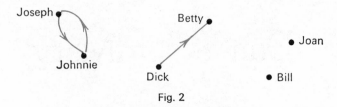

Fig. 2

Dick is the brother of Betty,
Joseph is the brother of Johnnie,
Johnnie is the brother of Joseph.

Copy Figure 2 and put in the other arrows that show 'is the brother of'.

Exercise B

1　In the family in Section 1, how many people have an uncle?

2　In a diagram like Figure 2, show all the members of the family that are necessary for the relationship

'is the uncle of'.

Complete the diagram by drawing all the arrows that indicate this relationship.

3　Draw diagrams with the sub-sets of people from Figure 1 and the arrows that indicate:

(a) 'is the father of';
(b) 'is the cousin of';
(c) 'is the brother of'.

4　What do the arrows in Figure 3 mean? What extra arrows have to be drawn to show the relationship represented by '=' in Figure 1?

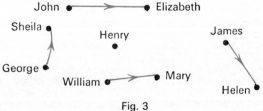

Fig. 3

5   Are there (i) always, (ii) never, or (iii) sometimes two arrows between
two people to show the relationship

(*a*) 'is the father of';
(*b*) 'is the cousin of';
(*c*) 'is the brother of'?

1.2   Other relations

The moon is above the clouds.
The post office is further away than the grocer's.
The judge is explaining the law.
The picture is being painted by John.

These sentences indicate relations between pairs of things. The
relations (we shall no longer use the word relationship) are

'is above',
'is further away than',
'is explaining',
'is being painted by'.

Exercise C

1   Write down three pairs of objects in the classroom which satisfy each
of the following relations:

(*a*) is in front of;   (*b*) is taller than;
(*c*) is older than;   (*d*) is owned by;
(*e*) is hidden by.

2   State at least two relations that hold between:

(*a*) you and your neighbour;   (*b*) you and your desk;
(*c*) you and your hands;   (*d*) an eagle and a sparrow;
(*e*) a ship and the sea.

3   The following are the ages of the children of the family in Figure 1:
Joseph, 17; Johnnie, 14; Betty, 15; Dick, 11; Bill, 6; Joan, 10.
Make an arrow diagram with this set of children and the relation 'is
younger than'.

4   Draw arrow diagrams to illustrate the relations:

(*a*) 'is greater than' on members of the set $\{1, 2, 3, 4, 5\}$;
(*b*) 'is 5 more than' on members of the set $\{1, 2, 3, 4, 5, 6, 7, 8\}$.

5   Draw an arrow diagram to illustrate the relations:

(*a*) 'is north of' on members of a set of cities;
(*b*) 'has more people than' on members of a set of countries;
(*c*) 'is the same shape as' on members of a set of your text-books.

1.3 Relations between sets

Make a list of, say, six boys or girls who sit near to you in the classroom, including yourself, and also a list of the different drinks they had yesterday. If a person had a particular drink, then we indicate this by drawing a line as in Figure 4.

For example, Dick had tea and lemonade.

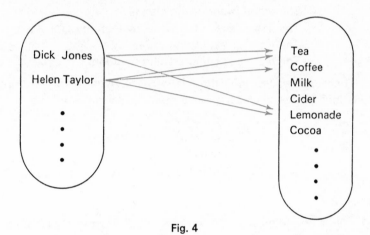

Fig. 4

Which was the most popular drink?
Who had the widest variety of drinks?
In this example, the members of two sets are linked by a relation.

In the same way, it is possible to have a relation between the members of two sets of numbers. For example, the set $\{2, 3, 5\}$ and the set $\{3, 6, 10, 15\}$ can have their members related by 'is a prime factor of'.

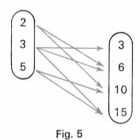

Fig. 5

Exercise D

1 List a set of family pets and another set of people you know. Use an arrow diagram to illustrate the relation 'is owned by'.

2 List a set of people you know and a set of television programmes. Draw arrows to illustrate the relation 'watched the programme'. Which was the favourite programme? Who watched the largest number of programmes?

3 Make a list of Junior schools in your area and some of the people in your class. Use an arrow diagram to show the relation 'used to be the school of'. Are there any schools from which especially large numbers have come? Why is this?

4 Draw arrow diagrams to represent the relations

(a) 'is the height of';
(b) 'is the age of';
(c) 'is the number of brothers of';

between suitable sets of numbers and some members of your class.

5 Draw a diagram to represent the relation 'is a factor of' between the members of {2, 3, 5, 7} and the members of {30, 31, 32, 33, 34, 35, 36}. Which number had no arrows joined to it? Why?

6 Draw a relation diagram between the members of {1, 2, 3, 4, 5} and the members of {30, 31, 32, 33, 34, 35, 36} to illustrate the relation 'is the number of prime factors of'.

2. MAPPINGS

If the members of the set {1, 2, 3, 4, 5} are each doubled, a new set is formed, {2, 4, 6, 8, 10}. Doubling transforms members of one set into members of the other. The transformation can be illustrated as an arrow diagram:

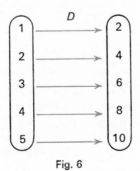

Fig. 6

We say that the members of one set are *mapped* onto the members of the other. Under the mapping, 4, for example, is called the *image* of 2. A mapping is a special kind of relation in which each member of one set is related to exactly one member of the set of images. (Figure 4 does not illustrate a mapping.)

We can imagine a mapping machine.

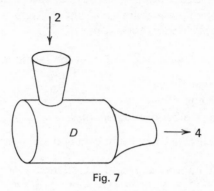

Fig. 7

When 2 is put into the machine, it is transformed into 4. The machine will double any number put into it. 4 is called the *image* of 2 under the mapping *D*. Notice that the machine can only produce one answer.

The following are also mapping diagrams. What is the machine doing in each case?

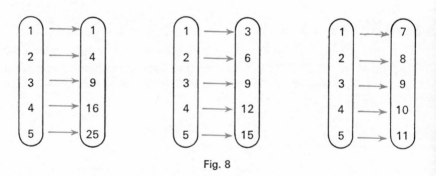

Fig. 8

If we let *x* stand for any member of the set {1, 2, 3, 4, 5} under the mapping shown in Figure 6, what is the corresponding member of the other set? We show the patterns of the mappings by using letters for numbers like this:

$$x \rightarrow 2 \times x,$$

which we usually write as $x \rightarrow 2x$.

The patterns for the mappings in Figure 8 are:

$$x \rightarrow x^2,$$

$$x \rightarrow 3x,$$

$$x \rightarrow x + 6.$$

Exercise E

1 Draw mapping diagrams to show $\{2, 4, 6, 8\}$ under the following mappings:

(a) $x \to x^2$; (b) $x \to x - 1$;

(c) $x \to 2x$; (d) $x \to 10 - x$.

2 Express the following mappings in the form $'x \to ?'$:

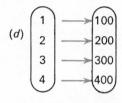

(a)

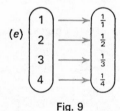

(b)

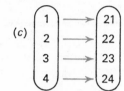

(c)

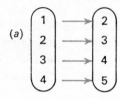

(d)

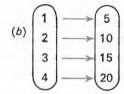

(e)

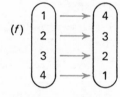

(f)

Fig. 9

3 What are the images of (a) 1, (b) 9, (c) 5, and (d) 0 under the mappings

(i) $x \to x^2$; (ii) $x \to x + 12$; (iii) $x \to 50 - x$?

4 What numbers have the following images under the mappings of Question 3:

(a) 36; (b) 49; (c) 16; (d) 25?

5 A square has rotational symmetry of order 4. The square $ABCD$ is rotated about its centre so that

$A \to D$; $B \to A$; $C \to B$; $D \to C$.

Through what angle has the square been rotated? On to what points are A, B, C and D mapped after an anticlockwise rotation of (a) a half-turn, and (b) a three-quarter-turn from its original position?

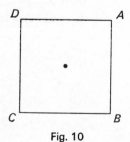

Fig. 10

87

3. ORDERED PAIRS

The relation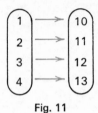

Fig. 11

can be represented as a set of ordered pairs, (1, 10), (2, 11), (3, 12), (4, 13). The pairs consist of the numbers at either end of each arrow.

The general expression for this relation is $x \to x + 9$. Write down the three ordered pairs for this mapping when it is applied to the numbers 5, 6, and 7.

Exercise F

1 Write down the ordered pairs that represent the relations:

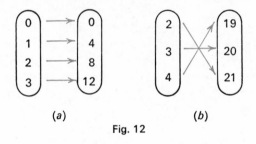

(a)   (b)

Fig. 12

2 Write down the ordered pairs that represent the mapping $x \to 4x$ applied to the set $\{10, 20, 30, 40\}$.

3 The following sets of ordered pairs are relations. State them in the form $x \to$? giving the set to which they are applied. For example, in (a), the mapping $x \to 3x$ is applied to the set $\{1, 3, 5, 7\}$.

(a) (1, 3), (3, 9), (5, 15), (7, 21);

(b) (1, 4), (3, 6), (5, 8), (7, 10);

(c) (2, 5), (3, 6), (4, 7), (5, 8);

(d) (7, 5), (6, 4), (5, 3), (4, 2);

(e) (2, 4), (3, 6), (5, 10), (7, 14);

(f) (1, 9), (3, 7), (6, 4), (10, 0).

4 The fact that a relation is a set of ordered pairs suggests that the relation can be shown on graph paper, using the first member of the pair to represent the x-coordinate and the second number to represent the y-coordinate.

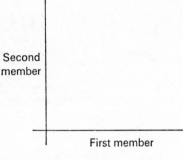

Fig. 13

Plot the ordered pairs of the six parts of Question 3. What do you notice about each set of plotted points? If lines were drawn through these plotted points, would any of them pass through the origin?

5 Work out the ordered pairs that show the following mappings applied to the set {1, 2, 3, 4, 5}. Plot the ordered pairs you obtain. Which sets lie on a straight line through the origin? Which do not lie on a straight line?

(a) $x \to 4x$;   (b) $x \to 4+x$;   (c) $x \to \dfrac{1}{x}$;   (d) $x \to 6-x$.

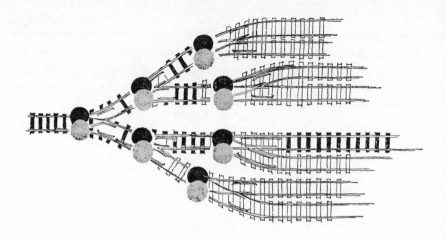

8. Binary and duodecimal bases

1. REVISION

In Book A we saw how we could do arithmetic in bases other than ten, and before going on with new work, some revision would be useful.

Exercise A

1 Copy and complete this cross number. Clues are given in base ten, give the answers in base five.

Across		Down	
1.	8	1.	49
3.	39	2.	19
6.	124	4.	66
7.	15	5.	20
8.	21	9.	87
9.	18	10.	103
11.	12	11.	11
12.	90	13.	19
14.	38		
15.	23		

Write your answers to the following questions in the given base.

2	$23_{five} + 14_{five}$	3	$45_{six} + 35_{six}$
4	$13_{four} + 32_{four}$	5	$133_{five} + 23_{five}$
6	$43_{six} - 15_{six}$	7	$32_{five} - 14_{five}$
8	$45_{six} \times 3_{six}$	9	$23_{four} \times 12_{four}$
10	$123_{eight} \times 14_{eight}$	11	$476_{nine} \times 10_{nine}$
12	$31_{five} \div 2_{five}$	13	$32_{six} \div 4_{six}$
14	$60_{eight} \div 10_{eight}$		

2. BASE TWELVE

We can make a spike abacus with spikes as tall as we like. Examine this one.

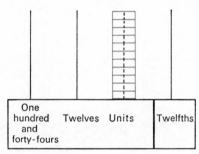

Eleven reels have been added to the units spike; if we try to add one more we shall have to change it and the eleven reels already on the units spike for a single reel on the next spike. This will stand for a group of twelve. We shall be counting in twelves.

The next three situations are easily represented in number symbols. But what about the last two?

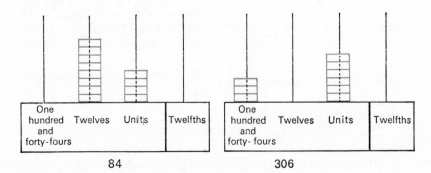

84   306

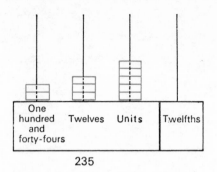

235

We want a single number symbol to represent the pile of reels on each spike, but we do not have a single symbol for the number ten or eleven.

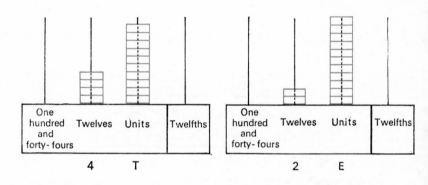

We shall have to invent new symbols for ten and eleven, and the simplest seem to be *T* and *E*.

Counting in base twelve will then go:

0, 1, 2, 3, 4, 5, 6, 7, 8, 9, *T*, *E*, 10, 11, 12, 13, and so on.

For example:

14_{twelve} is really

twelves	units
1	4

which is sixteen in base ten.

$2E_{\text{twelve}}$ is really two twelves and eleven units, which is thirty-five in base ten.

(Notice that this does *not* mean that 2 is multiplied by *E*.)

Exercise B

1 Copy and complete this table.

	Base ten	Base twelve
a	15	
b	20	
c	21	
d	30	
e	22	
f	36	
g	11	
h	58	
i	47	
j	144	

2 Copy and complete this table.

	Base ten	Base twelve
a		11
b		40
c		T
d		1E
e		51
f		60
g		3T
h		T0
i		E9
		TE

3 Copy and complete this addition table in base twelve.

+	0	1	2	3	4	5	6	7	8	9	T	E
0												
1												
2												
3												
4												
5												
6												
7												
8												
9												
T												
E												

Do not forget to look for patterns.

4   Make out and complete a multiplication square in base twelve.

The next questions are in base twelve, give your answers in base twelve also.

5	$57 + 28$	6	$39 + 28$
7	$36 + 46$	8	$67 + 55$
9	$79 + 1T$	10	$T0 + 1T$
11	$T0T + 11$	12	$147 + 307$
13	$36 - 19$	14	$65 - 28$
15	$77 - 39$	16	$81 - 22$
17	46×2	18	$1T \times 3$
19	$12 \times T$	20	$TE \times 10$

21
$$\begin{array}{r} T1E \\ + \, T0E \\ \hline \\ \hline \end{array}$$

22
$$\begin{array}{r} T0E \\ \times \quad 5 \\ \hline \\ \hline \end{array}$$

23 Try to explain the difference between working in the old units, feet and inches, and working in base twelve. Make up some examples to illustrate your points.

2.1   Bases greater than twelve

We have seen that we can make the abacus spikes as long as we like, so that we can work in bases greater than ten, and we took base twelve as an example. Even greater bases would be possible if we invented more number symbols.

For example, if we used base fourteen then we would need symbols for ten, eleven, twelve and thirteen. We could use T, J, Q, K. Counting in base fourteen would then go:

0, 1, 2, 3, 4, 5, 6, 7, 8, 9, T, J, Q, K, 10, 11, 12, 13, 14, 15, 16, 17, 18, 19, $1T$, $1J$, $1Q$, $1K$, 20, and so on.

Exercise C

1 (*a*) Invent the extra number symbols needed to work in base sixteen.

   (*b*) Write out the numbers from nought to thirty-two in base sixteen, using the symbols you have invented.

2 All these questions are in base sixteen and answers are also required in base sixteen.

          (*a*) 49 + 23;   (*b*) 36 + 44;

          (*c*) 25 + 46;   (*d*) 48 + 57;

          (*e*) 38 + 28;   (*f*) 19 + 38;

          (*g*) 18 + 49;   (*h*) 38 × 2;

          (*i*) 27 × 3.

3 What is the difference between working in base sixteen and working in the old units, pounds and ounces? Try and explain this in your own words and illustrate your answer with examples.

3. BASE TWO

The shortest spike we can put on the abacus is one that will take only one reel. Any attempt to put on two means we have to change spikes.

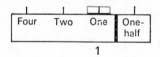

1

1 represents one

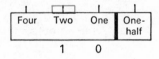

1   0

10 represents two

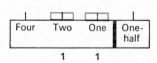

1   1

11 represents three

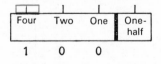

1   0   0

100 represents four

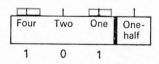

1   0   1

101 represents five

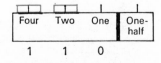

1   1   0

110 represents six

Binary and duodecimal bases

Exercise D

1 Imagine you had a very long abacus like this one and only one reel would go on each spike.

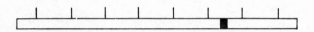

Make a copy of this abacus and write the name given to each spike in the space beneath it.

2 What are the only digits that can be used in this base?

3 Copy and complete this table.

	Base ten	Base two
a	3	
b	5	
c	10	
d	12	
e	15	
f	20	
g	25	
h	26	
i	30	
j	32	

4 Copy and complete this table.

	Base ten	Base two
a		10
b		100
c		111
d		1001
e		1100
f		1110
g		1000
h		10001
i		11111
j		100000

5 Copy and complete these addition and multiplication tables in base two.

(*a*)

+	0	1
0		
1		

(*b*)

×	0	1
0		
1		

96

6 All these additions are in base two, give answers also in base two.

(a)   1010
    + 101
   ─────

(b)   101
    + 1
   ─────

(c)   110
    + 101
   ─────

(d)   111
    + 1
   ─────

(e)   11100
    + 1011
   ─────

(f)   10101
    + 1101
   ─────

(g)   100001
    + 1101
   ─────

(h)   1111
    + 1
   ─────

(i)   1111
    + 11
   ─────

(j)   10101
    + 10101
   ─────

(k)   11001
    + 1111
   ─────

(l)   110011
    + 1110
   ─────

7 All these subtractions are in base two, give answers also in base two.

(a)   111
    − 11
   ─────

(b)   101
    − 11
   ─────

(c)   100
    − 1
   ─────

(d)   110
    − 1
   ─────

(e)   110
    − 11
   ─────

(f)   1010
    − 11
   ─────

(g)   10111
    − 1001
   ─────

(h)   11100
    − 10111
   ─────

(i)   110011
    − 11111
   ─────

8 All these multiplications are in base two, give your answers in base two.

(a) 101×10;

(b) 111×11;

(c) 1001×100;

(d) 1101×101;

(e) 10110×110;

(f) 10010×111.

9

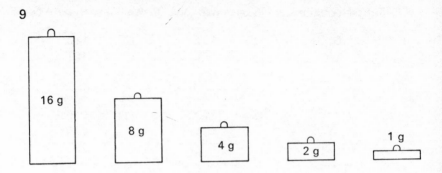

If you had this set of masses, list how you would find the masses of the quantities in the right-hand column.

Two examples have already been done for you.

16 g	8 g	4 g	2 g	1 g	Grammes
					1
					2
					3
					4
		1	0	1	5
					6
					24
					25
					26
1	1	0	1	1	27
					28
					29
					30
					31

3.1 The human computer

To make this, five (or more) pupils should stand out at the front and face the class, with both hands at their sides. These people form the 'calculating unit'. One other member of the class is needed as the 'input device'.

Numbers are fed into the computer by the input pupil, who makes a signal such as a rap on the desk or a single hand-clap. The computer counts every pulse which is fed into it in base two.

A alters at every pulse, 'If she is down she goes up and if she is up she goes down'.

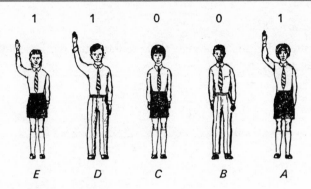

B alters at every second pulse.

C alters at every fourth pulse.

D alters at every eighth pulse.

E alters at every sixteenth pulse.

The computer illustrated above will count up to thirty-one, but more people can be added if required. It is best to start with just three people and keep adding extra people as everyone gets used to the idea.

3.2 Electronic computers

Base two is often called the 'Binary System' or the 'Binary Code' and it has become important because of its use in computers. Electronic computers depend on the flow of electric current.

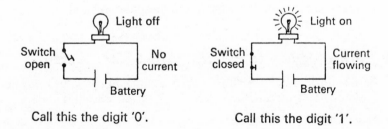

Call this the digit '0'.   Call this the digit '1'.

A row of light bulbs can be set up to represent numbers in the binary system; if the light is on call it '1' and if it is off, call it '0'.

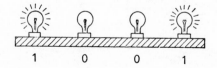

Exercise E

1 Write down the binary numbers represented by these lights and convert your answers to base ten.

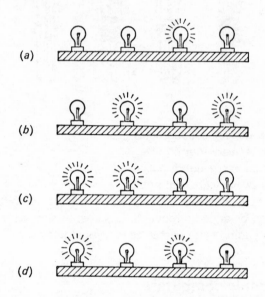

2 Illustrate these base ten numbers by lights in base two.

(a) 3;   (b) 6;   (c) 11;   (d) 15.

3 What is the largest number that can be represented by 4 lights? How many lights would you need to represent one hundred?

3.3 DIBS (device to illustrate the binary system)

Here is the circuit for a simple device you could make for yourself.

Materials: 4 bulb holders, 4 bulbs, 4 on-off switches, a battery, some wire and a base board.

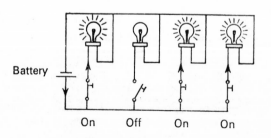

You do not have to restrict yourself to just four lights; more can be added if desired.

The circuit on p. 100 will illustrate numbers in the binary scale up to fifteen, but it will not add, carry or do any other arithmetical processes. Circuits which will do this are more complicated and depend on special switches, relays and transistors.

3.4 Computer tape

A representation of base two numbers can easily be made by punching holes in a piece of paper tape. This is how numbers are fed into some computers. There are different ways of doing this and a simplified way is dealt with here.

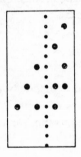

A hole stands for the digit one.

No hole stands for zero.

Exercise F

1 Write down the numbers in base two represented by these tapes. Convert your answers to base ten. Ignore the small holes, they are just to drive the tape through the machine.

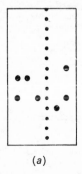

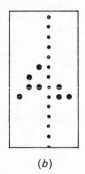

(a)   (b)

2 What is the largest number you can represent with this five-hole tape?

3 Words can also be put on to computer tape by first numbering the letters of the alphabet from one to twenty-six in base two. What does this tape say?

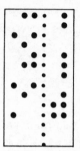

4 Make a drawing of a piece of paper tape which has your name on it in a pattern of holes as suggested in Question 3, and stick it on the front of your mathematics exercise book.

4. BASE TWO FRACTIONS

Going back to the idea of a base two spike abacus, we remember that the spare spikes stood for fractions or parts of units. We used a 'point' to show where the whole numbers ended and the fractions began.

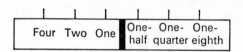

Exercise G

1 Copy the table and put the answers in. The first three have already been done for you.

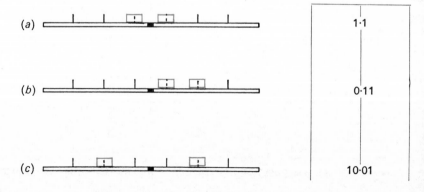

(a)   1·1

(b)   0·11

(c)   10·01

(*d*)

(*e*)

(*f*)

(*g*)

(*h*)

2 All these are in base two, give answers also in base two.

(*a*) + $\begin{array}{r} 10\cdot 1 \\ 1\cdot 1 \end{array}$ (*b*) + $\begin{array}{r} 110\cdot 011 \\ 11\cdot 01 \end{array}$ (*c*) + $\begin{array}{r} 111\cdot 0101 \\ 11\cdot 1011 \end{array}$

(*d*) + $\begin{array}{r} 10\cdot 001 \\ 11\cdot 111 \end{array}$ (*e*) − $\begin{array}{r} 11\cdot 11 \\ 1\cdot 01 \end{array}$ (*f*) − $\begin{array}{r} 101\cdot 101 \\ 1\cdot 111 \end{array}$

(*g*) − $\begin{array}{r} 10\cdot 011 \\ \cdot 101 \end{array}$ (*h*) − $\begin{array}{r} 10\cdot 101 \\ 1\cdot 011 \end{array}$ (*i*) $1\cdot 01 \times 10$

(*j*) $11\cdot 0 \times 11$ (*k*) $11\cdot 011 \times 100$.

3 These additions are in base two, give answers also in base two.

(*a*) + $\begin{array}{r} 1110\cdot 01 \\ 101\cdot 11 \\ 100\cdot 01 \end{array}$ (*b*) + $\begin{array}{r} 101\cdot 101 \\ 11\cdot 11 \\ 1\cdot 0011 \end{array}$

Binary and duodecimal bases

Exercise H (Miscellaneous)

1 Copy and complete these number scales for addition in base two.

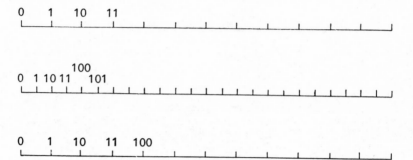

2 Draw a diagram to show how the scales are used to add 1001 to 11.

3 Copy and complete this base two cross-number.

Across

1. $1011 + 11$	1000. $10000 \div 100$
101. $1110 \div 10$	1010. $100 - 1$
110. $1 + 1$	1011. $111 - 10$
111. $10 + 1$	1101. 111×11

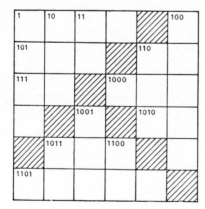

Down

1. 111×10
10. $1 + 10 + 100$
11. $1 \cdot 1 \times 10$
100. $1101 + 110$
110. $11 + 10$
1001. $1111 - 1010$
1011. $0 \cdot 1 + 0 \cdot 1$
1100. $100 \div 10$

4 All these questions are in base twelve, give your answers also in base twelve.

(a) $29 + 37$;   (b) $46 + 6$;   (c) $25 + 27$;

(d) $T + T$;   (e) $T \times 2$;   (f) 12×11.

5 Design a set of addition scales which will work in base twelve.

6   8 Great-grandparents   4 Grandparents

            2 Parents   1 Person

Here is part of your family tree; you should recognize the pattern of numbers by now.

(a) How many great-great grandparents do you have?

(b) How many great-great-great-great grandparents have you?

7 These numbers are written in base ten, convert them to base two.

(a) 9;   (b) 14;   (c) 21;   (d) 26;   (e) 31;   (f) 63.

8 These questions are in binary; give your answers in binary.

(a) $10101 + 1011$;   (b) $1001011 + 11100$;

(c) $1010000 + 110001$;   (d) $1101 - 111$;

(e) $1000 \cdot 101 - 0 \cdot 111$;   (f) 101×101.

9. Statistics

1. A SURVEY

Let us imagine that a Headteacher wants to find out how his pupils come to school and how many use each method of travel.

Some will walk, some cycle, others come by train, and so on, and the Headteacher must first decide which headings to group pupils under. He might decide to try:

Walk　Cycle　Bus　Train　Brought by Car

Already there are difficulties, and decisions will have to be made.

What about the pupil who has a long walk from the bus stop? Does he come under the heading 'Walk' or 'Bus', or should we make a new heading?

What about the girl who cycles when it is fine weather but who is brought by car when it is raining? You can probably think of other difficulties as well.

The Headteacher will probably decide to put these 'awkward' cases into the group they belong to most frequently, although in many cases this might not be an easy decision to make.

This means that the results will not give a perfectly accurate picture of the situation. Two people faced with the same decision might decide differently.

Here is the result of a survey made on a class of first-form boys and girls to find out how many are using each method:

walk, 13; cycle, 8; bus, 4; train, 9; car, 2.

We can just write the results out like this, or we could try to find a way to display them so that they were easier to follow, or even to see at a glance.

The first method suggested is a simple table:

Walk	Cycle	Bus	Train	Car	
13	8	4	9	2	Total 36

The total has been included and this acts as a useful check.

2. BAR CHARTS

Another simple way to display this information is on a 'Bar Chart'.

How 1 a come to school

Notice: (i) The chart has a heading.
　　　　　(ii) The words 'Number of Pupils' show what the numbers stand for.
　　　　　(iii) The bars are not touching.

A bar chart can be drawn sideways if you like:

How 1 a come to school

In this case it is easier to write the words in the actual bars.

Exercise A

1 Carry out a survey of the way in which people in your own class travel to school. You should have a short discussion first to agree on headings and what to do with 'awkward' cases.

Present your information both as a table and as a bar chart which you can colour.

2 See if you can obtain the same information as in Question 1 from another First Form which is the same size as yours, and compare results.

3 Would you expect any great difference between the results from your form and those from a fifth form? Try to obtain details from a senior form and compare them with yours.

4 Decide on headings to cover 'How my day is spent': for example, 'Working', 'Travelling', 'Eating' and so on. Try to avoid having more than 8 headings. Having decided upon headings which will be the same for all the class, each pupil should find out how long he spends on each activity and display his results in a bar chart.

Problems arising:

(*a*) Shall we all do the same day?

(*b*) Should we choose a working day or holiday?

5 Make a list of all the subjects on your time-table and the number of minutes spent on each in the course of the week. Display these results in the form of a bar chart.

3. PIE CHARTS

Another simple way of displaying the relation between the different methods of travel and the numbers who use them, is by means of a 'Pie Chart'.

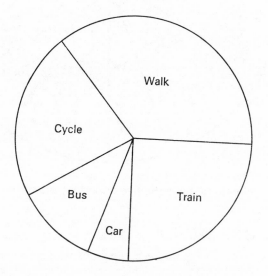

Walk	Cycle	Bus	Train	Car	
13	8	4	9	2	Total 36

Take the results of the survey on coming to school on p. 107. Each of the 36 pupils has to have an equal share of the pie. If 36 pupils share 360° then each one should have 10°. In degrees, the table will be:

Walk	Cycle	Bus	Train	Car	
130	80	40	90	20	Total 360

Use your protractor to check the above diagram.

If a large pie chart is made then everybody's name can be included:

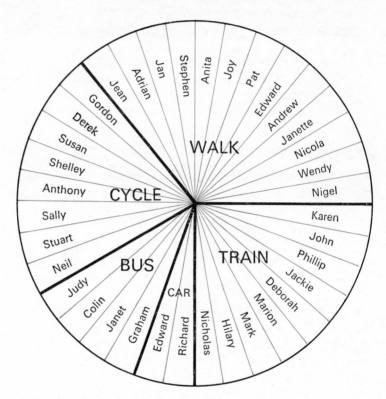

Colours will help to make the five important sectors stand out.

4. PICTOGRAMS

How 1 a come to school

Car	☺ ☺
Train	☺ ☺ ☺ ☺ ☺ ☺ ☺ ☺ ☺
Bus	☺ ☺ ☺ ☺
Cycle	☺ ☺ ☺ ☺ ☺ ☺ ☺ ☺
Walk	☺ ☺ ☺ ☺ ☺ ☺ ☺ ☺ ☺ ☺ ☺ ☺

An attractive way of representing information is the *pictogram*. In this, little drawings are used to display the details.

A stencil, lino-cut or potato-cut can be used to help produce these diagrams.

Compare this chart with the sideways bar chart on p. 108.

Exercise B

1 Make a pie chart of the results of the survey on 'Travelling to school' in your class. Remember that 360° have to be shared out equally by the total number of pupils in the survey.

2 Make a pie chart to show 'How my day is spent'.

3 Show your results to Exercise A, Question 5, as a pie chart.

4 During one month, this is the way a man spent his money:

	£
Rent	24
Rates	4
Heating	8
Lighting	4
Food	20
Drink	6
Clothing	5
Travel	8
Entertainment	11

If all these items were represented separately on a pie chart it would look too complicated and lose its effect. Group together (Rent and Rates), (Heating and Lighting), and (Food and Drink), and then make a pie chart.

5. PROJECTS

1. A vehicle survey

What could you do to convince people that there ought to be a pedestrian crossing and a crossing patrol warden outside your school?

If a case is to be presented to the authorities it would be better if it was backed by details of the sort of vehicles that passed and their numbers, so a proper traffic survey is called for.

Many things have first to be decided and much preliminary discussion will be needed.

Points for discussion and decision are:

(*a*) Which day of the week will you choose? Remember early closing.

(*b*) What time of day will you choose?

(c) For what length of time will you count vehicles?

(d) Will you repeat the experiment over many days, say a week?

(e) Will you just do the same day each week for four weeks?

(f) Where will you stand?

(g) Will you count traffic in one direction only or in both?

(h) How will you classify the types of vehicle?

(i) How will the weather affect things?

(j) Is it necessary to produce a form for recording results?

(k) Is a trial run desirable?

Having decided on all these points, and any others which might arise because of the special circumstances of your school, you are ready to do the actual survey. Here is a suggested form:

VEHICLE SURVEY

Name .... Date ....

Location .... Time started ....

Direction .... Time finished ....

Weather conditions ....

	TALLY	TOTAL
Motor cars and vans		
Lorries and large commercial vehicles		
Buses and coaches		
Motor cycles, mopeds, scooters		
Pedal cycles		
Other vehicles (with description)		

Others could be—Fire engines, tractors, police and military vehicles, horses and carts, ambulances, steam rollers, etc.

The attempt to classify cars and vans into one group and lorries and large commercial vehicles into another might lead to some difficulties which you will have to try to overcome.

Results:

(i) A neat and completed form can serve as a table.

(ii) Produce a bar chart.

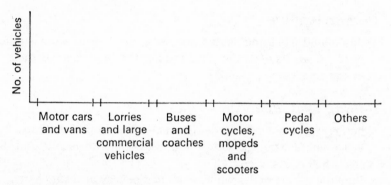

(iii) Display as a pie chart.

(iv) Display as a pictogram.

2. *The most common letter*

Aim: To list the order of frequency of letters in an English book.

Method:

(*a*) Decide on a book which every member of the class has.

(*b*) Assign a page to each pupil.

(*c*) List the alphabet and tally off through the page.

(*d*) Pool results.

Results:

(*a*) Display as a table from A to Z.

(*b*) Re-arrange the table and list the letters in order of frequency.

(*c*) Display as a bar chart in order of frequency.

Why is a pie chart unsuitable?

Conclusions:

What is the most common letter you have discovered?
Would this have been the same if you had chosen any other book?
Can these facts be put to use by anybody?

3. The most common letter in French

Repeat Project 2 but use a French book.

4. The most common length of word

Carry out a survey to discover the most common length of word in a book, following the lines of Project 2.

How do you think the result depends upon the type of book chosen?

5. Rolling one die

Roll a die 60 times and list the number of times each score is obtained.
Pool the results of all the class and display them as a bar chart.
Is any conclusion possible?

6. Rolling two dice

When two dice are rolled together, scores can range from 2 to 12.
Work with a partner, one to roll and the other to record, and roll two dice for half a lesson.
Pool the results of the whole class and display as a bar chart.
What about a conclusion?

Miscellaneous Exercise

1   Describe the data shown in this bar chart. How many families are involved? How many children?

Draw a similar chart for the families represented in your class. Discuss whether the same shape would be expected for a similar class 100 years ago.

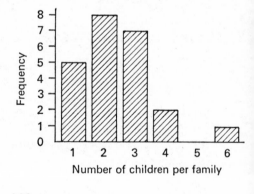

2   A shopkeeper sold fireworks at various prices. There were 1p ones, 2p ones, etc. He kept a record of the first 60 fireworks bought one day as follows:

1p	1p	6p	3p	2p	3p	6p	9p	2p	4p	2p	4p
6p	2p	1p	4p	9p	5p	4p	1p	2p	2p	1p	4p
5p	3p	3p	3p	9p	6p	1p	3p	6p	4p	1p	5p
2p	4p	6p	2p	3p	2p	1p	1p	9p	6p	2p	1p
1p	2p	6p	1p	5p	3p	1p	1p	9p	1p	2p	1p

(*a*) Put these results into a table, using tally marks to show how many of each type were sold.

(*b*) Display these results as a bar chart.

(*c*) Which firework was the most popular?

3 A musical survey in form 2*Z* revealed the following facts about the popularity of certain recording groups.

12 liked the Earwigs best of all,   3 liked the Popalongs,

9 liked the Caterwaulers,   2 liked the Squareboys.

4 liked the Crotchet String Quartet,

Illustrate this information by drawing:

(*a*) a bar chart;   (*b*) a pie chart;

(*c*) devise some other method of showing the information.

4 Make a frequency table for the letters occurring in the following place-name:

LLANFAIRPWLLGWYNGYLLGOGERYCHWYRNDROBWLL-
LLANTYSILIOGOGOGOCH

Which are the four most frequently appearing letters? In which country do you think this place is?

5 The numbers of principal farm animals in Great Britain are:

cattle, 12 million;   sheep, 30 million;   pigs, 6 million.

Draw a pie chart to illustrate this information and state the angle of each 'slice' in degrees.

6 Draw a suitable pictogram to illustrate the following figures, giving the value in hundreds of thousands of £'s of herring landed in English and Welsh ports in the years shown:

1952	...	15	1955	...	10
1953	...	$14\frac{1}{2}$	1956	...	10
1954	...	13	1957	...	9

7 Copy this table and see how many points you can list:

Bar chart		Pie chart	
Advantages	Disadvantages	Advantages	Disadvantages

115

Interlude

'SHIFTS'

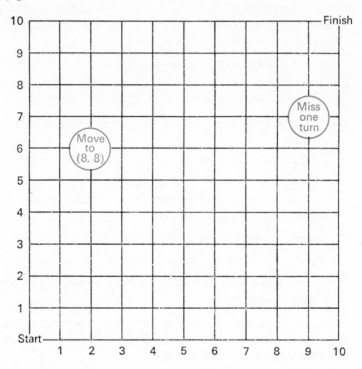

For the game of 'Shifts' you need: squared paper marked as shown, two small cubes and some counters. The cubes should be marked

$$X0, \quad X1, \quad X2, \quad X3, \quad X4, \quad X5$$
and $\qquad Y0, \quad Y1, \quad Y2, \quad Y3, \quad Y4, \quad Y5.$

Two or more people can play, each one taking turns at throwing the two marked cubes and at moving their counters. The numbers marked on the cubes state the distance to be moved or 'shifted' towards the right and towards the top of the board. A player at (2, 1) who throws (X1, Y4), moves to (3, 5). A player at (8, 9) with this throw would move to (9, 9) ignoring the Y shift that takes him beyond the edge of the board.

Four or five more instruction boxes should be added before starting the game. The object of the game is to move from the start (0, 0) to the finish (10, 10) before the other players.

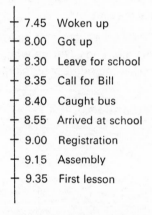

10. Directed numbers

1. REFERENCE POINTS

1.1 Time-tables

Here is a time-table showing part of a schoolboy's morning.

7.45	Woken up
8.00	Got up
8.30	Leave for school
8.35	Call for Bill
8.40	Caught bus
8.55	Arrived at school
9.00	Registration
9.15	Assembly
9.35	First lesson

Fig. 1

As the boy finds it difficult to get up and get to school on time, he has a time-table pinned up above his bed. In order to help him get there on time, he wants to know how many minutes he has left before 'zero hour', that is, Registration Time. His time-table therefore looks like this:

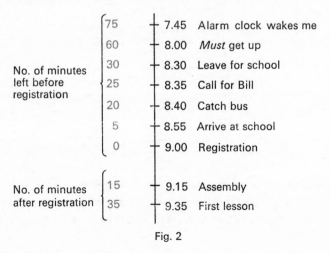

No. of minutes left before registration
75	7.45	Alarm clock wakes me
60	8.00	*Must* get up
30	8.30	Leave for school
25	8.35	Call for Bill
20	8.40	Catch bus
5	8.55	Arrive at school
0	9.00	Registration

No. of minutes after registration
| 15 | 9.15 | Assembly |
| 35 | 9.35 | First lesson |

Fig. 2

Directed numbers

Exercise A

1 (a) Copy Figure 1 into your book and leave space to put the following events in their correct place:

   (i) 8.15: breakfast;
   (ii) 8.25: clean shoes;
   (iii) 8.50: get off bus;
   (iv) 9.10: go down to Assembly;
   (v) 9.30: Assembly finishes.

   (b) Taking arrival time at school as 'zero hour', show the number of minutes left before arrival or the number of minutes after arrival, for each event.

2 Draw up a time-table as in Figure 1 showing what you do yourself in the mornings. Decide what will be your 'zero hour' and for each event put in the number of minutes before or after this zero hour.

1.2 Distances

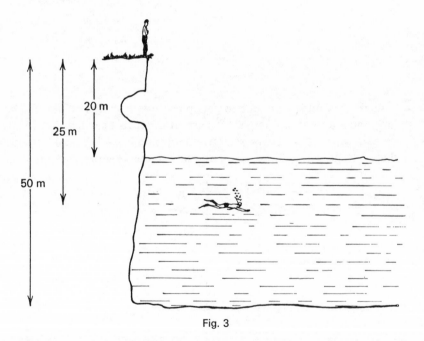

Fig. 3

Figure 3 shows a man at the top of a 20 m cliff.

The numbers show the distance in metres of certain objects below his feet. For example, sea level is 20 m below him, while a skin diver is 25 m below him.

Copy Figure 3 but instead of making the top of the cliff your 'zero' or 'reference point' make sea level your zero and put in the number of metres above or below it of the top of the cliff, the skin diver and the sea bed. Mark in also

(*a*) a cave, 10 m below the cliff top;

(*b*) the head of the man, 2 m above the cliff top;

(*c*) another diver, swimming 5 m above the sea bed.

1.3 Class project on ages

Find out the ages to the nearest month of each person in your class. Taking your own age as your 'reference point' or 'zero', write down the ages of everybody else as so many months older than or younger than yourself.

You may find it easier if you first rewrite your list of names in order of age, with the youngest first and oldest last.

Exercise B

1 Copy Figure 3 again but this time make the entrance to the cave your zero reference point.

2

Mountains	Height above sea level (m)	
Scafell Pike	980	
Snowdon	1100	
Ben Nevis	1340	
Slieve Donard	850	
Carrauntoohil	1040	0

Copy this table which shows the heights of the highest mountain in each country of the British Isles.

(*a*) Taking Carrauntoohil as your zero, calculate in the heights above and below this reference point.

(*b*) Choose any other mountain you like as your zero. Add another column to your table and fill in the heights of the other mountains above and below this new reference point.

3 If we know how far north or south of the Equator a place is, we can begin to describe its position. In this case, we use the Equator as our zero. For example, Nottingham is 53° N, York is 54° N, Newcastle is 55° N, Edinburgh is 56° N, Londonderry is 53° N, Southampton is 51° N.

Taking York as your zero, write down the position of these places north and south of this new zero.

4   In describing the positions of various places, a line through the Poles and Greenwich is taken as zero. A place is so many degrees west or east of this line. For example, Liverpool is 3° W, Birmingham is 2° W, Swansea is 4° W, Portsmouth is 1° W, Canterbury is 1° E, Glasgow is 4° W, and Belfast is 6° W.

Taking a line through Birmingham as your zero, write down the position of the other places, including Greenwich, west and east of this new zero.

5   Figure 4 shows the average body temperatures of some species of animal, measured on the Celsius scale. Copy the table and show the number of degrees Celsius that each of these temperatures is above or below the body temperature of man.

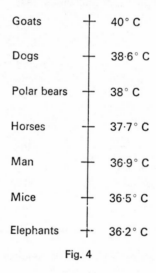

Goats	40° C
Dogs	38·6° C
Polar bears	38° C
Horses	37·7° C
Man	36·9° C
Mice	36·5° C
Elephants	36·2° C

Fig. 4

2. DIRECTED NUMBERS

In the examples of the previous section, all measurements were made from a reference point, sometimes called the 'zero'. Any point can be chosen as a zero; it is a matter of convenience.

We have used words such as 'before' and 'after', 'above' and 'below', 'east' and 'west', 'north' and 'south', 'younger' and 'older'. These words tell us the direction of other readings on either side of the zero.

This pattern appears again and again so a new set of numbers has been invented. This set can be used in all these situations and is called the set of 'directed numbers'. Numbers on one side of the zero will be called positive and will carry a '+'; numbers on the other side will be called negative and will carry a '−'.

For example, on Figure 2 with the zero at 9.00, arrival at school can be taken as ⁻5 and Assembly as ⁺15. In Figure 3, taking the top of the cliff as zero, the man's head is at ⁺2 and the sea level at ⁻20.

Sometimes it does not matter which direction is taken as positive and which as negative. If the man's head is taken as ⁻2, what would the sea level be? But on some occasions, it is customary to accept one direction as positive. All the temperatures on Figure 4 are positive. How would you give the temperature at which a salt solution freezes if this is 23° below zero?

2.1 Class project on heights

Find out the heights to the nearest centimetre of each person in your class. Taking your own height as your zero, write down the heights of everybody else in relation to your own. Use positive numbers to show the number of centimetres taller than yourself and negative numbers to show the number of centimetres shorter than yourself. You may find it easier to rewrite your list of names in order of height with the smallest first and the tallest last. Make a plan of your final result using a line like the one in Figure 5.

Exercise C

1 Copy Figure 4. Take the average body temperature of man as your zero and mark the other points on the scale using positive numbers for points above your new zero, and negative numbers for points below.

2 The height of John's house is 100 m above sea level. Describe the heights of the following objects in relation to John's house:

    (*a*) a television mast 800 m above sea level;

    (*b*) a church   220 m above sea level;

    (*c*) a boat at sea   0 m;

    (*d*) a bridge   85 m above sea level;

    (*e*) a submarine   40 m below sea level.

3 (*a*) If 9 o'clock is zero hour for your arrival at school in the mornings, express the following arrival times in minutes making use of the extended number system. (For example, a quarter to nine is ⁻15 min.)

(i) 3 min to 9 o'clock;   (ii) 5 min past 9 o'clock;   (iii) 8.50 a.m.

(*b*) What would your answers be if the zero hour were 8.55 a.m.?

4 The average age of a class is 12 years 3 months.

(*a*) Judith, John, Jack and Jim are 12 years, 11 years 10 months, 12 years 7 months, and 11 years 8 months old respectively. How do their ages differ from the average?

(*b*) Barbara, Betty, Benjamin and Bill have ages which, when related to the average, are ⁻9 months, 0 months, ⁺3 months, and ⁻5 months. What are their ages?

(*c*) Name two members of the class with the same age.

3. THE NUMBER LINE

We have already met the number line as in Figure 5 made up of the counting numbers and zero.

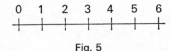

Fig. 5

Suppose we now wish to extend the number line to the left of zero. This will give us numbers on both sizes of zero. In order to be able to tell the difference between them, we can use the positive and negative signs. The numbers to the right of zero will carry the positive sign and the numbers to the left of zero will carry the negative sign, as in Figure 6.

Fig. 6

If you have done the class project on heights properly, you will have already shown the information you have gathered on a number line. Check to see whether it is correct.

Now show the information gathered on class ages on a number line, with your own age as your zero.

On your number line for class heights, one person is represented by ⁺3, and another by ⁻2. Which is the taller?

On your number line for class ages, one person is represented by $^+1$ and another by $^-4$. Which is the older?

In the Celsius scale of temperature, which is hotter, $^-20°$ or $^-30°$? Which is smaller, $^-5$ or $^+3$? (see Figure 6).

The answers to all these questions depend on the *order* of the numbers. On the number line, shown in Figure 6, $^-5$ is smaller than $^+3$ because $^-5$ is to the left of $^+3$. You have already met a symbol showing this order relation 'is smaller than', namely '$<$'. So we write

$$^-5 < {}^+3.$$

Mark the numbers on a number line and find out which of the following statements are true.

(a) $^-2 < {}^-4$;   (b) $^-4 < {}^-1$;   (c) $^-1 < {}^+3$.

We can write these last two relations together as

$$^-4 < {}^-1 < {}^+3$$

because $^-1$ is to the left of $^+3$ and to the right of $^-4$.

Give some possible values for x if:

(a) $x < {}^-3$;   (b) $^-6 < x < {}^+5$;   (c) $^+1 < x < {}^+2$.

Exercise D

1 Write each pair of numbers with the smaller first, for example, $^+2 < {}^+5$:

(a) $^+3, {}^+7$;   (b) $^+4, 0$;   (c) $^+4, {}^-2$;

(d) $0, {}^-3$;   (e) $^-1, {}^-3$;   (f) $^-5, {}^-3$.

2 Arrange the following numbers in order, smallest first:

$$^-3, {}^+2, {}^-5, {}^+7, {}^+6, {}^-8, {}^-10.$$

3 Copy each pair of numbers and put in the correct sign, (either $<$ or $>$) between them:

(a) $^+4, {}^+6$;   (b) $^+5, {}^+3$;   (c) $0, {}^+6$;

(d) $^-3, 0$;   (e) $^-4, {}^+2$;   (f) $^+5, {}^-3$;

(g) $^-2, {}^-3$;   (h) $^-5, {}^-1$;   (i) $^-1, {}^+1$.

4 Give two possible values of x if:

(a) $x < {}^+10$;   (b) $^+7 < x$;   (c) $x < {}^-4$;

(d) $^-8 < x$;   (e) $x > {}^+2$;   (f) $^-3 > x$.

5   Part of the set of points for which $x < {}^{+}5$ can be shown on a number line in the following way:

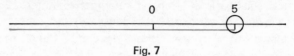

Fig. 7

The circle shows that the point ${}^{+}5$ is not included in the set. In a similar way, show on the number line the sets of points for which:

(*a*) $x < {}^{+}3$;　　　(*b*) $x < {}^{-}1$;　　　(*c*) ${}^{+}2 < x$;

(*d*) ${}^{-}3 < x$;　　　(*e*) $x > {}^{-}5$;　　　(*f*) ${}^{+}1 > x$.

6   Give a value for *x* if:

(*a*) ${}^{+}2 < x < {}^{+}9$;　　(*b*) ${}^{-}3 < x < 0$;　　(*c*) ${}^{-}7 < x < {}^{-}4$;

(*d*) ${}^{-}2 < x < {}^{-}1$;　　(*e*) ${}^{+}5 > x > {}^{+}1$;　　(*f*) ${}^{-}3 > x > {}^{-}6$.

11. Topology

1. TOPOLOGICAL TRANSFORMATIONS

Look carefully at the drawings in Figure 1.

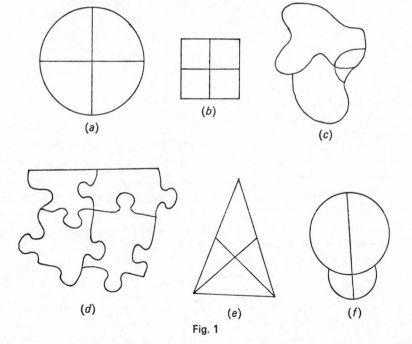

(a)

(b)

(c)

(d)

(e)

(f)

Fig. 1

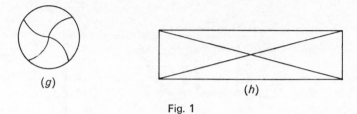

(*g*) (*h*)

Fig. 1

(*a*) Make a list of the ways in which the drawings differ from one another. *Example*: some drawings are made entirely from segments of straight lines; others are not.

(*b*) Make a list of the ways in which the drawings are alike. *Example*: each drawing divides the page into the same number of cells or regions.

Imagine Figure 1 (*b*) to be drawn on a very thin rubber sheet. This can be pulled and twisted about as much as you like so long as you do not tear the rubber or stick two pieces together.

Figure 2 shows Figure 1 (*b*) drawn on a rectangular piece of rubber sheet which is pulled about so that the drawing looks like Figure 1 (*a*).

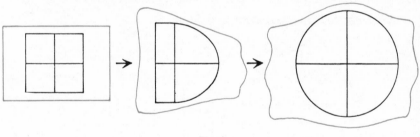

Fig. 2

Topology is about points, lines and the figures they make; but length, area, curvature and angle can be altered as much as you wish. Thus topology is sometimes called rubber-sheet geometry.

(*c*) Figure 3 shows a piece of wire netting. Suppose it to be twisted—even stretched—but not torn or fixed together. After this it will be a different shape; it may not be flat. But some things will remain unchanged. What are these? What differences will there be? Discuss your answers with your neighbour or your teacher.

Fig. 3

(i) We call bending and stretching (but not tearing or sticking) *topological transformations*.

(ii) Facts that are still true about a drawing or network after it has been transformed are called *invariant* because they do not change or vary. The order of points on a line is invariant. The distance between two points is not invariant.

(iii) Two curves such that each is a topological transformation of the other are said to be *equivalent*.

Exercise A

1 A topological transformation of a circle is called a *simple closed curve*. Which of the drawings in Figure 4 are simple closed curves? (*Reminder*: you may not cut or stick.)

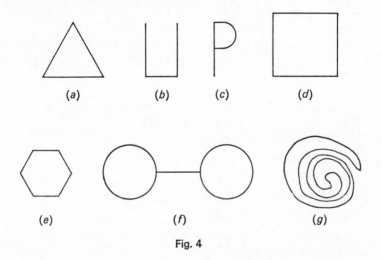

Fig. 4

2 Can the first curve of each pair in Figure 5 be transformed topologically into the second curve?

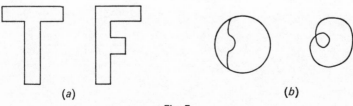

Fig. 5

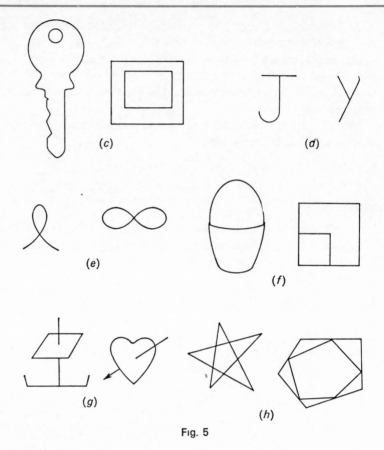

Fig. 5

3 Which of the curves in Figure 6 are topologically equivalent to the straight line segment *AB*?

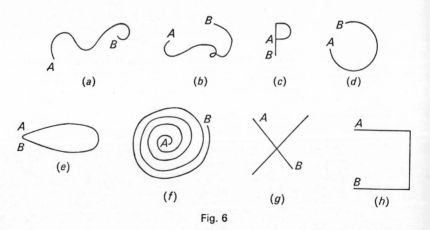

Fig. 6

4 Which of the drawings in Figure 7 are topologically equivalent to each other?

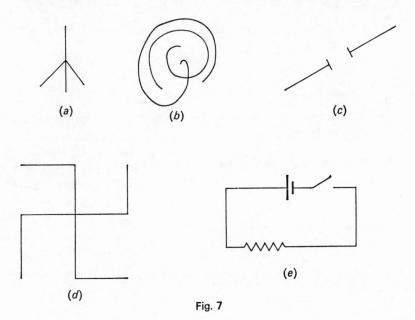

Fig. 7

5 Which of the pairs of drawings in Figure 8 are equivalent? If you think a pair is equivalent, copy the second member of the pair and mark on it a possible position for *A'*, the image of *A* under the transformation. If more than one position is possible, mark all of them. You are allowed to turn the figures over.

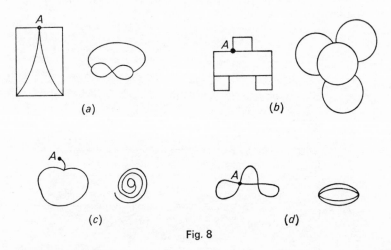

Fig. 8

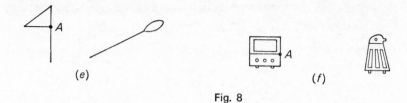

Fig. 8

Will any of your answers be different if you are not allowed to turn the figures over?

6 What can you turn a beetle into? The original insect and two suggestions are shown in Figure 9.

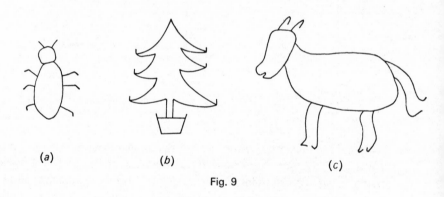

(a)　　　　　(b)　　　　　(c)

Fig. 9

7 Draw some topological transformations of each of the drawings in Figure 10.

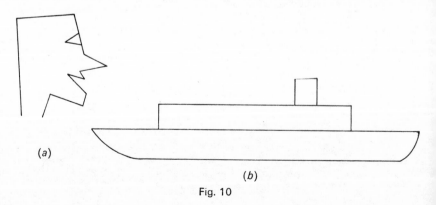

(a)

(b)

Fig. 10

(*d*)

(*c*)

Fig. 10

2. NODES

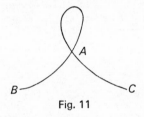

Fig. 11

(*a*) Look at Figure 11. There are four paths from the point *A*. One leads to *B*; where do the others lead?

(*b*) How many paths are there from *C*?

A point with at least one path leading from it is called a *node*. The *order* of the node is the number of paths. *A* is a 4-node because there are four paths from *A*.

(*c*) Describe the node at *C*.

(*d*) State the order of each node marked with a letter in Figure 12.

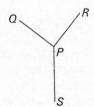

Fig. 12

131

Exercise B

1 Make a list of the letters in Figure 13 which have, amongst others:
   (*a*) one 3-node;   (*b*) two 3-nodes;   (*c*) one 4-node.

a b c d e f g h i j k l m n o p q r s t u v w x y z

Fig. 13

2 Why is it impossible to draw a figure with one 1-node and no other nodes?

3 Draw a line segment. Mark a 2-node on it. Mark another one. How many are there altogether?

4 Copy and complete the following table for the networks in Figure 14.

Figure	Total number of nodes	Number of 1-nodes	Number of 3-nodes	Number of 4-nodes	Number of 5-nodes
(*a*)					
(*b*)					
...					

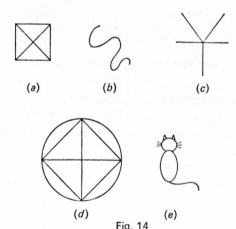

(*a*)   (*b*)   (*c*)

(*d*)   (*e*)

Fig. 14

5 Which of the letters in Figure 13 are topological transformations of the letter *c*? How many nodes has each of these letters? What kind of nodes are they?

6 Which of the letters in Figure 13 are equivalent to the letter *y*?

Investigation 1

Draw, if possible, figures which have:

	1-nodes	3-nodes	4-nodes	5-nodes
(a)	—	—	2	—
(b)	—	1	1	1
(c)	—	3	—	—
(d)	—	2	1	—
(e)	1	1	—	1
(f)	4	—	1	—
(g)	—	2	2	—
(h)	1	1	—	—

Make up some more examples of your own. When is it impossible to draw a figure? Try to find a rule for deciding whether or not a figure can be drawn.

3. ARCS AND REGIONS

A line joining two nodes is an *arc*. An area bounded by arcs is a *region*. The area outside a figure is also a region. Each of the networks in Figure 15 has 4 nodes, 6 arcs and 4 regions. (2-nodes are not counted. Why?)

 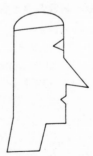

Fig. 15

Investigation 2

(a) Using some of the networks in Figure 16 and others of your own, make a table showing the number of nodes (N), arcs (A) and regions (R) in each of the networks. (Do not count 2-nodes.)

(b) Ask your neighbour to check your results.

(c) Look for patterns in your table. Comment on these patterns.

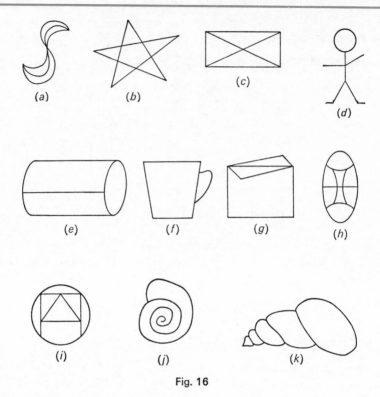

Fig. 16

4. TRAVERSABLE NETWORKS

A figure is said to be *traversable* if it can be drawn with one sweep of the pencil, without lifting the pencil from the paper, and without tracing the same arc twice. It is permitted to pass through nodes several times. The networks in Figure 17 are traversable.

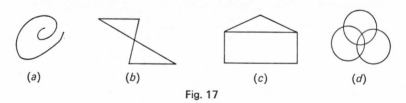

(a)   (b)   (c)   (d)

Fig. 17

Exercise C

1   Make rough sketches of the drawings in Figure 17 to show that they are traversable. Mark the point where you start (*S*) and the point where you finish (*F*).

2   Draw three traversable networks of your own, showing the start and finish.

3   Draw a traversable network with two 1-nodes and no other nodes. Where can you start and finish? Can you start from more than one point? Can you draw a network with just two 1-nodes which is not traversable?

4   Draw a traversable network with two 4-nodes and no other nodes. Where can you start and finish?

5   Which of the networks in Figure 16 are traversable? You may have to try several starting points before you either succeed or decide that the network is not traversable.

Investigation 3

Investigate possible starting and finishing points in traversable networks. When is a network traversable?

Investigation 4

The drawings in Figure 18 are not traversable. What is the least number of strokes in which each can be drawn? Compare your answers with those of your neighbour.

Add another line to Figure 18 (*d*). Do you now need fewer strokes, more strokes, or the same number of strokes? Does your answer depend on which extra line you draw?

How many extra lines must you add to Figure 18 (*a*) in order to make it traversable?

Draw other figures of your own. What is the least number of strokes in which each can be drawn? Can you find a rule for deciding how many strokes you need by just looking at a figure?

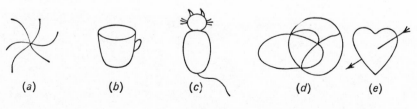

(*a*)   (*b*)   (*c*)   (*d*)   (*e*)

Fig. 18

5. INSIDE OR OUTSIDE

Fig. 19

Investigation 5

(*a*) Figure 20 shows a simple closed curve and two points *A* and *B*. Which point is outside the curve? Can you reach *B* from *A* without crossing the curve?

(*b*) Figure 21 also shows a simple closed curve and four points *W, X, Y, Z*. Which of the four points are inside the curve? How can you tell?

(*c*) Draw other simple closed curves. There is one in Figure 19. Try to find a rule for deciding which points are inside your curves.

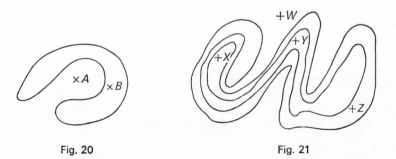

Fig. 20   Fig. 21

6. COLOURING REGIONS

(*a*) Copy the networks in Figure 22. Colour them so that regions with a common arc have different colours. Do not forget the outside region! (Regions with a common node may have the same colour, so long as they do not also have an arc in common.) Try to use as few colours as possible. State the number of colours you need in each case.

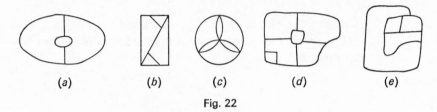

(*a*)　　　　(*b*)　　　　(*c*)　　　　(*d*)　　　　(*e*)

Fig. 22

(*b*) Draw networks of your own which need:

   (i) only two colours;　　　　(iii) at least four colours.

   (ii) at least three colours;

Can your neighbour colour any of your networks with fewer colours than you have used?

(*c*) Can you find a map that needs at least five colours?

(*d*) Draw a map with eight regions which needs only three colours.

No design has yet been found which needs more than four colours. It has been proved that no more than five colours are needed; it seems that four will do, but this is a result which has yet to be proved—or disproved !

If you think you have found a map which needs five colours, see if some-one else can colour it in four. If not, you will have made mathematical history.

Exercise D

1　Copy the patterns in Figure 23 and colour them using as few colours as possible.

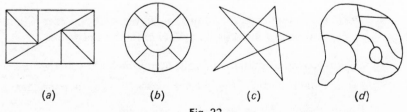

(*a*)　　　　　(*b*)　　　　　(*c*)　　　　　(*d*)

Fig. 23

2 Trace a map of northern or southern England showing the counties, and colour it with four colours. How many are usually used in an atlas?

3 Draw a unicursal curve, that is, a continuous line which comes back to its starting point. It may cross itself as often as you like, but you must not re-trace an arc already drawn (see Figure 24).

How many colours do you need to colour the regions of your design?

Compare your answer with those obtained by other members of your class. What can you say about the colouring of regions formed by unicursal curves?

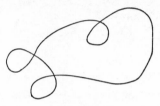

Fig. 24

4 Draw the tessellations shown in Figure 25 and colour them using as few colours as possible.

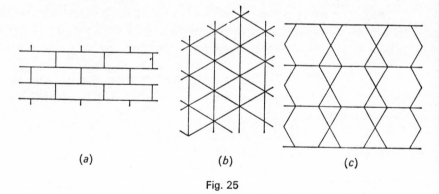

(a) (b) (c)

Fig. 25

5 Draw some of the eight semi-regular tessellations (see Chapter 2, p. 21) and colour them using as few colours as possible.

6 Design repeating patterns of your own which are suitable for:

(a) a kitchen floor; (b) a book jacket; (c) a wallpaper.

Colour them using as few colours as possible.

Summary

A *topological transformation* allows twisting and stretching but not tearing or joining.

An *invariant* under a topological transformation is a fact about the original figure which is still true about the new one.

Two curves are topologically *equivalent* if one can be transformed into the other by a topological transformation.

A *simple closed curve* is equivalent to a circle.

A *node* is a point with at least one path leading from it. The order of a node is the number of paths.

A line joining two nodes is an *arc*. Every point of an arc is a 2-node with the exception of its ends.

An area bounded by arcs is a *region*. The area outside a figure is also a region.

A figure is *traversable* if it can be drawn with one sweep of the pencil, without lifting it from the paper and without tracing the same arc twice.

Here is a list of the invariant facts we have already met. (Dashed letters are used for the points and lines into which the original ones are twisted and stretched.)

(*a*) If a point *P* lies on a line *l*, then *P'* lies on *l'*.

(*b*) If P_1, P_2, P_3 lie in that order on *l*, then P'_1, P'_2, P'_3 lie in that order on *l'*.

(*c*) If there are *n* paths from *P*, then there are *n* paths from *P'*. In Figure 26 (*c*), there are eight paths from *P*.

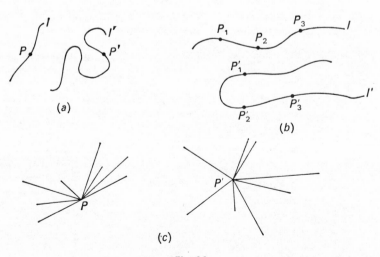

(*a*)

(*b*)

(*c*)

Fig. 26

It is not possible to draw a figure which has an odd number of odd nodes.

For any figure, $N + R = A + 2$, where N = number of nodes, R = number of regions and A = number of arcs.

A figure is traversable if it has: (*a*) two odd nodes, (*b*) no odd nodes. It may have any number of even nodes.

A line segment that starts outside a simple closed curve and finishes inside cuts the curve in an odd number of points.

Networks are coloured so that regions with a common arc have different colours. No one has yet found a plane design which needs more than four colours.

Exercise E (Miscellaneous)

1 Which of the following are simple closed curves:

(*a*) an equilateral triangle;   (*b*) an octagon;
(*c*) a letter *N*;   (*d*) a figure 8;
(*e*) a letter *R*?

2 Would you consider 'inside' and 'outside' to be topological invariants?

3 The parallelogram *ABCD* is transformed into the square *EFGH*. Is it always, sometimes or never true that:

(*a*) $A \to E$, $B \to F$, $C \to G$, $D \to H$;
(*b*) $A \to E$, $B \to G$, $C \to F$, $D \to H$;
(*c*) $A \to G$, $B \to F$, $C \to E$, $D \to H$?

4 (*a*) Two figures are equivalent. Must they have the same number and order of nodes?

(*b*) Two figures have exactly the same number of nodes of the same order. Must the figures be equivalent?

5 Classify the networks in Figure 27 into topologically equivalent sets.

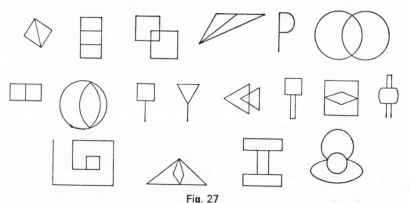

Fig. 27

6   Figure 28 shows a topological
map of some roads. How many
cross-roads are there? How many
junctions are there?

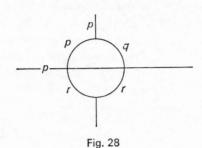

Fig. 28

The three sections marked *p*
actually form a straight road
running SW–NE. The section *q* is
winding but runs roughly N–S.
The sections *r* form a straight road
running E–W. Sketch your idea of
what the map really looks like.
Mark the *p*'s, *q*'s and *r*'s on your
sketch.

7

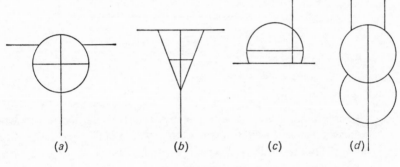

(a)   (b)   (c)   (d)

Fig. 29

Look carefully at the drawings in Figure 29. Which of them are
possible topological maps of the roads shown in Figure 30?

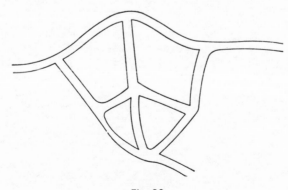

Fig. 30

8 Figure 31 shows a plan view of a small bungalow. Can you start at *A* and walk through every door of the bungalow exactly once?

(*Hint*: mark a dot in each room and a single dot outside, join the dots with lines so that one line passes through each door, and consider the network you have now drawn.)

Can you start anywhere except *A* and succeed in traversing the network?

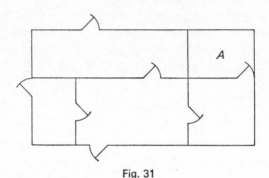

Fig. 31

9 *The Koenigsberg problem.* In 1737 the famous Swiss mathematician Leonard Euler was working at the court of Catherine the Great of Russia. He was asked to solve the problem of the bridges of Koenigsberg. This town is now found on maps under the Russian name of Kaliningrad. There are two islands in the River Pregel which runs through the town. Seven bridges cross the river as shown in Figure 32.

The problem was this: is it possible to take a walk which crosses each of the bridges once and once only? Euler solved the problem by changing it into a problem about the nodes of a network. See if you can solve the problem.

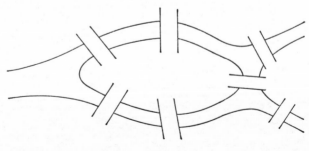

Fig. 32

10 Draw a circle of radius 5 cm. Draw
a straight line from one point on
the circle to another (see Figure
33 (*a*)). There are now two inside
regions and the inside can be
coloured with two colours.

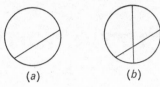

(*a*) (*b*)

Fig. 33

Draw a second straight line so as to make as many new regions as
possible (see Figure 33(*b*)). How many regions are there? How
many colours are now needed to colour the interior? Draw a third
straight line to make as many new regions as you can. Continue the
process and enter your results in a copy of the following table:

Number of lines	Number of regions	Number of colours
0	1	1
1	2	2
2		
3		
.		
.		
.		

Look for patterns in your table and comment on those that you find.

11 *The colour game.* This is a game for two players. The first player draws
a region. The second player colours it and draws a new region. The
first player colours this region and adds a third. The game continues
until one of the players is forced to use a fifth colour; this player is the
loser. Play this game with a friend.

Investigation 6

Figure 34 shows a 'crossed-
over' pentagon with one
one crossing. Can you draw
crossed-over pentagons
with 2, 3, 4, 5 crossings?
What can you say about
crossed-over hexagons?
Investigate the numbers of
crossings which are possible
in crossed-over polygons.

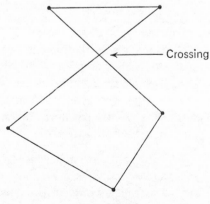

Crossing

Fig. 34

Puzzle corner

$$+\begin{array}{c} \text{CROSS} \\ \text{ROADS} \\ \hline \text{DANGER} \end{array}$$

Each letter stands for a number. If O represents 2 and S represents 3, what do the other letters represent?

2   In how many different ways can a pair of dice land?

3

$$\times\begin{array}{c} BC \\ BC \\ \hline ABC \end{array}$$

What numbers do A, B and C represent?

4   How can 6 identical match sticks be arranged to form 4 equilateral triangles?

5   Among twelve similar coins there is one 'fake' which weighs less than the others. Explain how, using only three weighings of a balance, you can find the fake coin.

6

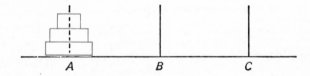

Three discs of different sizes are arranged as shown in the figure. We wish to transfer all the discs, one at a time, on to spike B, so that they are arranged in the same way. (At no time is it permitted to place a larger ring over a smaller one, but you can of course use spike C.) What is the smallest number of moves necessary to complete the transfer from A to B?

7   The words in capitals in (a)–(d) form an anagram (another word made from the same letters), in each case a single mathematical word. The other words give a final clue. For example, 'LARGE TIN with three sides' would be TRIANGLE.

(*a*) BRAINY; a system of counting numbers.

(*b*) NO CAR—IT BUST; we certainly find a difference.

(*c*) I DO NOT CARE, and this helps to make the position clear.

(*d*) NO RICE LEFT: that's the effect of a mirror.

8 The diagram shows a simple ground floor plan of a house. Could you walk through this house so that you walked through each door once and once only?

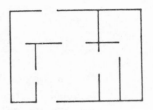

   (*Hint*: make a topological drawing by making each room into a node and each door into an arc.)

9 Two men and 2 boys want to cross a river but they only have a canoe which will carry 1 man or 2 boys. How do they get across?

   (*Hint*: the figure shows the first stage.)

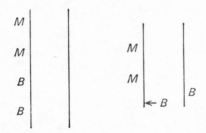

10 A man goes to a barrel with 2 jars; one holds 3 litres and the other 5 litres. Explain how he can measure 4 litres.

11 Plot the points (2, 0), (2, 2), (2, 4), (3, 2), (4, 0), (4, 2), and (4, 4). Draw five line segments each containing three of these seven points.
    Now find two more points which will enable you to draw four more line segments each containing three of the new total of nine points.

12 Ten pennies are placed in a row touching one another. Any penny may be moved over *two* of those next to it on to the coin beyond. How can you move the coins in this way so that they will be arranged in equally spaced pairs?

    (*Hint*: move only those coins in odd positions *or* only those in even positions.)

13 Use all the numbers from 1 to 9 once each to form three equivalent fractions as in the following example:

$$\frac{2}{4} = \frac{3}{6} = \frac{79}{158}.$$

145

14

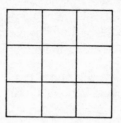

Using a copy of the figure, arrange the set of numbers from 1 to 9 in the small squares, called cells, so that if you add the numbers written in any row or column, or diagonal, you will always obtain the same answer. (Square arrays of numbers with these properties are known as 'Magic Squares' and were known to the Chinese over 2000 years ago.)

Revision exercises

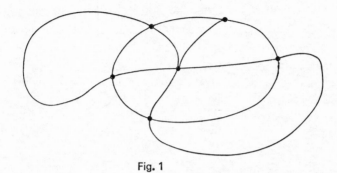

Fig. 1

Quick quiz, no. 3

1 Is Figure 1 traversable?

2 A line joins (3, 0) to (3, 6). What is its equation?

3 Subtract 1 from the following numbers:

    (a) 100_{two};   (b) 350_{six};   (c) 1000_{eight}.

4 Work out the following:

    (a)   £   (b) $
        2·37   4·82
        5·88   −   1·99
  + 0·90

5 What are the bearings of

    (a) A from B;

    (b) B from C;

    (c) A from C;

    (d) C from A?

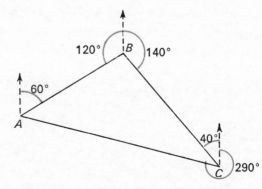

6 On to what set is {2, 4, 6, 8} mapped by the following:

(a) $x \to 3x$; (b) $x \to \frac{1}{2}x$?

Quick quiz, no. 4

1 State which of the following figures are topologically equivalent to each other:

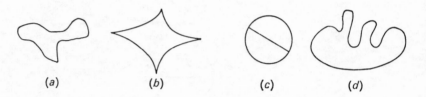

(a) (b) (c) (d)

2 Add 1 to the following numbers:

(a) 1011_{two}; (b) 102_{three}; (c) 144_{five}.

3 Give a possible value for x if

(a) $x > {}^{-}2$; (b) $x < {}^{+}1$;

(c) ${}^{-}4 < x < 0$; (d) ${}^{-}7 < x < {}^{-}2$.

4 What is the final bearing after

(a) start facing SE and do an anticlockwise turn of 110°;

(b) start facing NW and do an anticlockwise turn of 280°;

(c) turning 170° clockwise from east?

5 What mapping in the form $x \to$? when applied to {2, 4, 6, 8} maps it on to

(a) {5, 7, 9, 11}; (b) {1, 3, 5, 7}?

6 What is the perimeter of a regular 12-sided polygon of side 2·5 cm?

Exercise C

1 Say which of the shapes (i)–(x) are topologically equivalent to each of the shapes (a), (b), (c) and (d).

(a) (b) (c) (d)

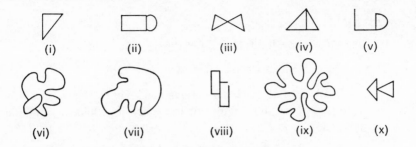

(i)   (ii)   (iii)   (iv)   (v)

(vi)   (vii)   (viii)   (ix)   (x)

2 Combine the following binary numbers:
   (*a*) 101101 + 1011100;   (*b*) 1011100 − 101101;
   (*c*) 10010 × 1101;   (*d*) 110110 + 101010 + 1111;
   (*e*) 111001 + 100111 − 1010.

3 Suppose the British and continental (24-hour) systems for recording
   the time are to be replaced by a new system in which 12 noon becomes
   'zero-hour' from which all times are measured, e.g. 2.30 p.m. (or
   14.30 h) would be written as $^+$2.30 and 7.15 a.m. would be $^-$4.45.

   (*a*) Convert the following to the new system:

   (i) 16.00 h;   (ii) 19.40 h;   (iii) 8.12 a.m.; (iv) 5.47 a.m.

   (*b*) Convert the following 'new' times to the continental system.

   (i) $^-$0.13;   (ii) $^+$9.08;   (iii) $^+$7.39;   (iv) $^-$11.18.

4 A yacht sails round a hexagonal course in a clockwise direction
   ABCDEF, each 'leg' of the course *AB*, *BC*, *CD*, . . . being 2 kilometres
   long. On what bearing is it sailing on each 'leg' if the first is due east?

5 A travel agency carried out a survey on the holiday habits of students.
   240 students who had not gone abroad were asked to state their main
   type of accommodation during their previous summer holiday. The
   results were as follows:

Type of accommodation	Number of students
Hotel, boarding house, etc.	50
Holiday Camp	29
At home or staying with friends	77
Caravan	18
Tent	30
Boat	25
Others	11
	240

Show this information on a pie chart.

Revision exercises

Exercise D

1 (*a*) Write down the following in descending order:

$$-9, \quad +6, \quad -5, \quad +3, \quad -1.$$

(*b*) The height of my house above sea level is 320 m. Use + and − signs to express the heights of the following objects in relation to my house:

(i) a radio mast 2200 m above sea level;
(ii) a church 320 m above sea level;
(iii) a bridge 210 m above sea level;
(iv) a submarine 100 m below sea level.

2 Draw an arrow diagram to show the relation 'is a factor of' between members of {2, 3, 4, 5} and members of {4, 6, 8, 10}.

If the direction of the arrows in your diagram was reversed, what relation would your diagram show?

Find a different relation between these two sets. (Write the answer in the form $x \rightarrow$?) Is this relation a mapping?

3 Sketch, if possible, figures with:

(*a*) One 4-node, one 3-node and one 1-node;
(*b*) one 5-node, two 3-nodes and one 1-node;
(*c*) one 1-node, one 5-node and one 4-node.

4 A girl is sitting on a beach. The entrance to the pier is 200 m away on a bearing of 310° and the end of the pier is 220 m away on a bearing of 337°. Find by accurate drawing the length of the pier.

A boat is moored 300 m away from the girl on a bearing of 040°. How far would someone have to swim from the end of the pier to reach the boat?

5 In this question,

$$\square = 10_{ten} \quad \boxed{1} = 11_{ten} \quad \boxed{2} = 12_{ten}$$

$$\boxed{3} = 13_{ten} \quad \text{etc.}$$

Find what number base is being used in each of the following calculations:

(*a*)	1 6 □	(*b*)	3 3 8	(*c*)	□ $\boxed{3}$ 3	(*d*)	4 0 2
	+3 3 3		−2 8 7		+9 1 6		−1 6 3
	4 □ 0		4 1		1 3 $\boxed{4}$ 9		2 4 □

150

Exercise E

1 Criticize the following statements:

(a) the distance from here to Oxford is 6·0251 km;

(b) my car is 1·73 m wide, so if the gate posts are about 1·75 m apart I'll be able to get through;

(c) we need 2·0371 g of butter for this cake;

(d) you just can't trust this newspaper—there were 999 people in the audience, but they reported it as 1000.

(e) you're supposed to dial 999 for the police, but I never do: 1000 is near enough for me!

2 The average number of ounces of sweets consumed per month by 14-year-old girls in seven different countries were once as follows: Australia 32, Canada 34, France 13, New Zealand 30, Italy 37, U.K. 26, U.S.A. 44.

(a) Show this information on a pie chart.

(b) Show this information by means of a pictogram.

(c) Which method is better? Why?

(d) Would it make any difference to your answer to (c) if all you wanted to do was to convince an unthinking English girl that she might slim more easily in France? Why?

3 Complete the following table.

	To 3 s.f.	To 2 s.f.	To 1 s.f.	To 1 dec. pl.	To 2 dec. pl.
7·191					
10·270					
0·526					
109·3					

4 Does this tessellation have rotational symmetry about any of the points *A, B, C, D*? Are there any (other) points about which the tessellation does have rotational symmetry? Sketch the figure and mark any such points. Mark also any lines of symmetry which the figure has.

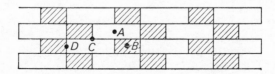

Revision exercises

5 Where necessary, complete the following arrow diagrams and state the relation that each illustrates. Each example is taken from a chapter in this book. For example:

Statistics

Method of travel   The number who use that method

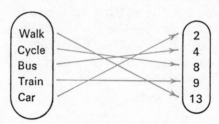

'Method of travel used by'

(a) *Relations*

?

(b) *Topology*

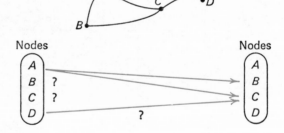

(c) *Angles*

Bearings   Clockwise rotations from north

'Gives the same direction as'.

Exercise F

Complete this cross-number

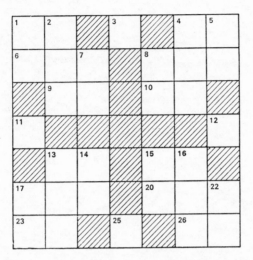

Clues across

1. The difference between the 4th and 8th prime numbers.
3. An octagon has ? lines of symmetry.
4. A 100-sided convex polygon has ? diagonals from any one vertex.
6. What is the angle (in degrees) of a regular pentagon?
8. 688 correct to 2 s.f.
9. The sixth triangle number.
10. What is the perimeter (in centimetres) of a rectangle measuring $13\frac{1}{2}$ cm by 11 cm?
11. $35-16 = 16$ is correct in what number base?
12. A tetrahedron has ? vertices.
13. Through how many degrees does the hour hand of a clock turn in 30 minutes?
15. If $A = \{1, 2, 3, \ldots, 40\}$ and $B = \{$multiples of 3 less than 60$\}$, how many members has $A \cap B$?
17. 12 dozen.
20. 214·499 correct to the nearest whole number.
23. How many fifths in four wholes?
25. A parallelogram has rotational symmetry of order ? about its centre.
26. $50\frac{6}{11}$ correct to the nearest whole number.

Clues down

1. There are ? prime numbers between 1 and 35.
2. 20_{ten} in base three.
4. The 500th positive odd number.
5. The product of the 1st, 3rd and 4th prime numbers.
7. The ninth square number.
8. 2^6.
13. 4 angles of a pentagon are each 100°. What is the fifth angle (in degrees)?
14. $64_{\text{ten}} = ?_{\text{twelve}}$.
15. A cube has ? edges.
16. Bearing of the NW direction.
17. A dodecagon has ? sides.
22. Total length (in metres) of the edges of a rectangular box measuring $2\frac{1}{4}$ m × 3 m × 5 m.

Published by the Press Syndicate of the University of Cambridge
The Pitt Building, Trumpington Street, Cambridge CB2 1RP
32 East 57th Street, New York, NY 10022, USA
296 Beaconsfield Parade, Middle Park, Melbourne 3206, Australia

© Cambridge University Press 1969

Library of Congress catalogue card number: 68–21399

ISBN 0 521 08357 5 hard covers
ISBN 0 521 07222 0 paperback

First published 1969
Reprinted 1970 1972 (twice) 1973 1974 (twice) 1976 1979 1981 1982

Printed in Great Britain at the
University Press, Cambridge